Behind the Smile!

Behind the Smile!

Richard W. Jenkins

Fresh Ink Group
Guntersville

BEHIND THE SMILE

Copyright © 2017
by Richard W. Jenkins
All rights reserved

Fresh Ink Group
An Imprint of:
The Fresh Ink Group, LLC
Box 931
Guntersville, AL 35976
Email: info@FreshInkGroup.com
www.FreshInkGroup.com

Edition 1.0   2017

Book design by Richard W. Jenkins

Cover by Stephen Geez

Except as permitted under the U.S. Copyright Act of 1976, no part of this publication may be reproduced, distributed, or transmitted in any form or by any means, or stored in a database or retrieval system, without prior written permission of the publisher.

Cataloging-in-Publication Recommendations:
POE023020 **POETRY** / Subjects & Themes / Love & Erotica
POE000000 **POETRY** / General
POE014000 **POETRY** / Epic

Library of Congress Control Number: 2017952404

Paper-cover ISBN-13: 978-1-936442-48-5
Hardcover ISBN-13: 978-1-936442-45-4
eBook ISBN-13: 978-1-936442-52-2

BEHIND the SMILE

Exceptional Poetic Renderings

of

Richard W. Jenkins

CONTENTS

Title		Page
Acknowledgements		xvii
Introduction		1
Chapter I — HOMAGE TO POETRY		**3**
I wonder why	English Sonnet	4
Dearly Beloved Pen of Mine	French Quatern	5
Ink	Blank Verse	6
Poets All	Unmetered Quatrains	7
Calling All Poets	Free Style	8
The High Road	English Sonnet	9
Chapter II — ROMANCE		**11**
Endless Life	Ballad	12
Gifting Stars	Quatrains	14
In that Moment	English Sonnet	15
Let's do it all again	Ballad	16
Memory's Gifts	Primetime	18
My Prayer	Ballad	19
One Desert Night	Pantoum	20
Our Psalms	Ballad	21
Out There	Quatrains in Mono-Rhyme	23
Sealed With A Kiss	Ballad	24
She loves me, too	Ballad	26

Springtime's Warm Embrace	English Sonnet	28

Chapter III — LIFE — 29

Come 'n Share	English Sonnet	30
Down on the Farm	Rhyming Couplets	31
Dusty Dirt Road	Unmetered Quatrains	33
I am a Man, and I am Free	Chant Royal	35
Life's Song	English Sonnet	38
Life's Sweet Music	Quickie	39
Marriage	Free Verse	40
Moving-time	English Sonnet	41
Poor man's lullaby	Quatrains	42
Streets of Houston	Crown Of Sonnets	43
Sweet, youthful years	Quatrains	51
Texas Wildfires	Fours 'n Eights	53
The Joys In Life	Chardelle	55
Three kinds of kids	Free Style	56
Til all life ends	English Sonnet	58

Chapter IV — LOVE — 59

Love	Free Verse	60
Attuned to Love	Ballad w/Envoi	61
Autumn and You	Rhyming Couplets	62
How you'll know I Love You	Sonnet Doublet	63
Lemon Avenue, Flowers and You	Free Verse	65
Love Psalm for My Lover	English Sonnet	67

Love's Pendulum	Mono-rhymed Verses	68
Loving You	Quatrains in 8-Count	69
Making Memories	English Sonnet	70
My darling golden rose	Ballad	71
Nighttime Reverie	Rime Royal	75
Pink Carnations, You 'n Love	Unmetered Quatrains	76
Soft tear	Ameri-Sonnet	78
Through Love	Brady's Touch	79
You Are My Seasons	Unmetered Quatrains	80
When, with love	Fours 'n Sixes	81

Chapter V — EMOTION — 83

What Would Life Be	Free Style	84
When You take the New Roads	English Sonnet	86
Wildflowers	Quatrains	88
Woken feelings	Freud Style	91
You might	Ballad	93

Chapter VI — IMAGERY — 95

A Peaceful Hush	Mollietta	96
Northern Lights	English Sonnet	98
These passion-filled dreams	Fives 'n Tens	99
Waking-up	Rhyming Couplets	100

Chapter VII — SADNESS — 101

Beside the pond	Free Verse	102
Blessed from above	Fives 'n Eights	104

In Eternity	Unmetered Quatrains	106
Lonely Boy	Unmetered Quatrains	108
Lost Fate	English Sonnet	109
Love's Ambling Seasons	Ballad	110
Lovers' Lament	Char's 3+1	112
Our Love's Seasons	Ballad	113
Sad Ink	English Sonnet	115
Softly ~ in my dreams	Kyrielle	116
The Dance	Unmetered Quatrains	117
Unacknowledged Phantom Lover	Free Verse	119
Whisper Of Shadows	Cywydd Devair Fyrion	122
Written with air	Free Verse	123

Chapter VIII_____HUMOR_____125

A Smile	English Sonnet	126
As I grew olde	English Sonnet	127
Conniption	Unmetered Quatrains	128
First Kiss	Unmetered Quatrains	130
Gobble! Gobble!	Unmetered Quatrains	134
Gud eatin'	English Limerick Doublet	136
Jus' Kuntry Fun	Two-Step	137
Lazy, Crazy, Mayzie	English Limerick	139
Lost Cookies	Unmetered Quatrains	140
Midsummer Dreamin'	French Quatern	142
Naughty 'n Nice	Rhyming Couplets	143

The Witch's Blush	Unmetered Quatrains	146
Wet Dream	Quatrains	147

Chapter IX — JAPANESE FORMS — 149

Blossom	Haiku	150
Dating Details	Senryu	151
fate	Sedoka	152
first taste	Tanka	153
God's canvas	Tanka	154
winter pages	Haiku Suite	155
Katana	Senryu	156
Life-thirst	Sedoka Doublet	157
lofty mantle	Haiku	158
meeting and departing	Tanka	159
the cure	Senryu	160
snowflakes falling	Senryu	161
seasons	Haiku	162
Death's Lure	Choka	163
You know something, gal?	Sedoka	164

Chapter X — PROMISE — 165

A Brand New Start	English Sonnet	166
at the altar of Your love	Unmetered Quatrains	167
Be At Peace	Skeltonic Verse	169
Breeze	Rhyming Couplets	170
Fate's Door	Tenzon 12	171

Gift us wings	Tripps O'er Quads	172
Missive from Your Muse	English Sonnet	173
Our Living Sea of Destiny	Quatrains	174
Remembrance	French Quatern	176
Seeking	Unmetered Quatrains	177
Sometimes	English Sonnet	179
Sweet Valentine	Rhyming Couplets	180
The Bluebird	Free Style	181
The Choice	Free Verse	183
The Flower In Your Hands	Free Verse	186
This Happy Song's for You	Unmetered Quatrains	188
Tho' Many Unfulfilled	Rhopalic Verse	190
To Be Your Man	Free Verse	191
Upon these words	Quatrains	193
When morning calls	Free Verse	195

Chapter XI_____SENSUALITY_____199

A-Wandering with You	Rhyming Couplets	200
all that I feel	Free Verse	201
Behind Closed Eyes	Parabolic Quatrains	203
Betwixt Your Charms	English Sonnet	204
Close soft thine eyes	Quatrains	205
Divine Treasures	English Sonnet	207
E'er gently eternal	Unmetered Quatrains	208
Endless Life	Ballad	210
Femme Coquette ·····—	English Sonnet	212

God's Paintbrush 'n Palette	Free Verse	213
Golden Crown	Concrete or Form Poetry	216
Heart to Heart	Eights 'n Sixes	217
How it used to be	Free Style	219
In Such Dreams	Eights 'n Sixes	221
I, These Quiet Places	Free Verse	223
Real love have I	Unmetered Quatrains	225
Secret Rendezvous	Quickie	226
Speak to Me	Rhyming Couplets	227
Sweetheart	Eights 'n Sixes	228
Tears of yesterday's longing	Spilling Ink	229
Tell it to the ochre moon!	Free Verse	230
We Soar, We Dream Forevermore	Quatrains	234
Wild flames of dreams	English Sonnet	236
Woman's Touch	Rhyming Couplets	237
Your Sweet Rain	Diminished Pentaverse	238

Chapter XII_____FANTASY_____241

An Angel's Love	English Sonnet	242
Daydreaming's Gifts	Primetime	243
Dream Lovers	Ballad	244
Dreams in Flight	Tenz 'n Eightz	245
Eden's Haven	Ballad	246
Green Eyes	Ballad	247
I Am...	Free Style	248
Ode to Vivid Dreams	English Sonnet	249

Robbie	English Sonnet	250
Recalling the Sky	Ottava Rima	251
save You!	Free Verse	252
Sweet Island Girl	English Sonnet	254
To vivid dreams	English Sonnet	255
When I hear your call	Quatrains	256
when you walk with me	Free Verse	257
Woodsprite	Villanelle	259
You Unmetered	Quatrains	260
You Awaken My Dreams	Free Verse	261
You're the One	Quatrains t	262

Chapter XIII_____THINKING_____265

A Simple Thought On Unity	Free Verse	266
Afterlife	English Sonnet	268
Better things to do	Ballad	269
Controversial Me	Free Verse	271
Consciousness	Free Verse	272
Desiree	Unmetered Quatrains	273
Enigma	Ballad	275
Freedom	Free Verse	277
Gotta Try	Unmetered Quatrains	278
Greater-self	Free Verse	279
I wonder Why	Blank Verse	280
If This Makes Any Sense	Eights 'n Sixes	281
In Life's Review	Unmetered Quatrains	282

In names unknown...	Child Four	283
Interrupting	Eights 'n Sixes	284
Islands	Concrete	286
Joy & Happiness	Free Verse	287
Karmic Relief	English Sonnet	288
Life's Bright Stream	Unmetered Quatrains	289
Life's Slaves	English Sonnet	291
Listen well, you who soar	Cinq Trois Decca La	292
Listen	Free Style	293
Mortality	Ruba'i	294
On Life and Death	Free Verse	295
On Motion	Prose	297
On Truth	Unmetered Quatrains	301
Paradoxical Infatuation	Parallelismus Membrorum	302
Path of Choices	Unmetered Quatrains	303
Self-made man	Prose Poetry	305
Some Kind of Advice	Prose Poetry	306
Sum of Industry	Prose	307
Take A Good Look	Unmetered Quatrains	308
Temple Knows	Unmetered Quatrains	310
The Other Way	Unmetered Quatrains	313
The Secret of Love and Wisdom	Prose	316
Us	Rhyming Couplets	317

Closing Comments_____318

List of Poetic Forms_____319

Acknowledgments...

The sort of man I've become, the poet that traveled along and developed with me, nor this book, could have been made possible without spending a large amount of my boyhood living from kinfolk to kinfolk, with no actual father-figure to follow or learn from.

Eventually, I grew-up throughout my formative and teen-hood years in the Houston, Texas, ghetto atmosphere, burgeoning under the ever-attentive scrutiny of a stern, hardworking mother and come-lately stepfather, that fed griping at me incessantly, deprived me of joy, and showed they cared by continually trying to whip and beat me into some sort of reasonable submission (misguided though they were). Alas, it just made me worse!

Then, there was my late mentor, Dr. Norman "Smitty" Smith, PhD ... bless his soul, whom without his guidance, I'm more than a bit certain I'd have ended up dead or in prison, like so many of my good ol' running buddies have.

Well, life moves-on, and I've no real complaints now, because life often has its own ways of reaching each of our minds, hearts, and souls, molding us into the beings we are, and though I'd not wish to live it again, I can say, with great gratitude, satisfaction, and appreciation, that I did not turn out too terribly twisted. Besides, it's all furnished a wealth of mental, spiritual, emotional, and intellectual treasure to draw from, for my trove of *literally* thousands of creative writings.

Therefore, I want to acknowledge my mother, whom I wish had lived to see her ne'er-do-well son become a published author, my stepfather, whom, in his own way tried; all my kinfolk, who practically raised me one at a time, and especially Aunt Kate, who taught me how to write my first poem at age nine ... bless her dear departed heart; I loved her so very much.

I cannot begin to repay uncountable numbers of friends I met along the way, with whom I shared life and gleaned untold treasures from ... and yes, you each know exactly who you are.

Then, there are all those marvelous women I fell in-love with; some I even married, and some I sired children with ... bless them one and all for opening my eyes, my heart, and my soul in such ways it has all turned to poetry. One marvelously special lady even taught me how to love ~*

Last, and definitely not least, there is Heidi, my dear, gorgeous, understanding, green-eyed, golden-haired, patient, kind, giving, gracious, and (most importantly to me) loving wife and friend, without whom this book would not now be in your hands.

A tome of gratitude and humbling acknowledgement is due to Stephen Geez and Ann Stewart, of publisher, Fresh Ink Group, who've applied their amazing skills, performing all the work necessary to design and format this book, *finally* getting my poetic renderings "out there". Many thanks to them for their endless patience and wherewithal in dealing with a tenderfoot, too; then, for going beyond the call, by teaching me the basic ins and outs of the publishing world.

Oh, yeah ... let's not forget life, Nature, love, the stars, and the universe!

"*Bless you and them – one and all!*"

Richard W. Jenkins
January 1st, 2017

Introduction

BEHIND the SMILE

Behind the smile – where dreams ensue,
lives a man whose bright mind dances.
Poems of life he writes ring true ...
sorrows, fancies, deep romances.

Of those whose tastes are varied wide,
there's something here for everyone.
You're sure to find so much inside,
to oo! and ah! with tears or fun.

One never knows what next he'll say,
or how his words will touch your soul;
but, it's for sure, if there's a way,
your heart, you'll find, he will have stole.

So, take a peek Behind the Smile;
a world you've never known before
awaits your pleasure for awhile ...
there's wonderment for you in store.

(Rhyming Quatrains in 8-Count)

HOMAGE TO POETRY

I wonder why?

(my first Sonnet, at age 9)

I watch the little ants when they crawl by.
The turtle and the snail each move real slow.
The spider made a web up there real high,
    The butterfly just flutters to and fro.

His name is Skip. He used to run and play,
And sleep each night beside me on the bed.
Then God came down and took my Skip away.
    Now I can hear him barking in my head.

I saw a dancing leaf fall on the ground,
And fluffy clouds are high up in the sky.
A brand new shiny penny I have found,
    Then I sit down alone and wonder why?

If I walk backward round the world today,
Will Skip be waiting here for us to play?

(English [Shakespearean] Sonnet)

~ Dearly Beloved Pen of Mine ~

Dearly beloved pen of mine,
so filled with flowing, golden verse
shines glowing luster ~ every line;
you dance so lightly, then coerce

each moment shared from love's repast.
Dearly beloved pen of mine,
release my thoughts, free them at last...
that I may savour life's sweet wine.

Today, tomorrow ... both entwine,
as sighing parchment waits ~ it yearns.
Dearly beloved pen of mine,
as one, we'll write the world that turns.

I heard your call ... you heed my voice,
upon this page, my hope's design;
you've spilt your ink, let us rejoice ~
Dearly beloved pen of mine.

(French Quatern)

…INK…

'Twas once I used to write; yet, naught in rhyme…
back there upon those youthful, bygone days;
it's been since then new forms have taken root,
with diff'rent ink my well-worn pen's now filled,
and swishes line to line – from page to page,
while often wild abandonment flows free.
Blank Verse and I (for many years) were one,
and now's returned to greet me this bright day.
Ah, who's to blame for ending this long drought?
It's my pal, Fanc E. Free … 'tis his fine name!
So, keep your pen close-by and well at hand,
else-wise you'll never know what will inspire,
and look at all that I'd been missing lest,
if we'd strayed far apart, as writers do;
and, here's a toast to you, my old friend, Ink,
for everyone here 'bout knows all you've done.
Since happiness you've always spread my way …
this votive verse – I now inscribe to You.

[Blank Verse]

POETS ALL

~ to the world's most special breed ~

Inside my frame
the poet doth dwell;
some will claim I am great,
others refrain, "A ne'er-do-well!"

Yet, it matters not
of me what they say,
as long as I can write and
faithfully express my own way,

that it's possible for
my thoughts to fly free,
take this old pen in my hand
release what the mind, it might see.

The soul, soaring high,
tells the heart what to feel;
when the head hears the heart,
desire and passions begin to unreel.

So, come all poets ...
where thy fantasy roams,
bring parchment, gold pens,
let's all write together the world's
most spectacular, spellbinding tomes.

(Unmetered Quatrains)

Calling All Poets!

Come all ye poets faire,
share your words
without care.

You're welcome here
from far and wide;
all your lovely friends,
invite for the ride!

Dip deep
your quills of gold,
into inkwells filled
by colors bold!

Stroke bright ~
let the fun begin ...
scribed in brilliant flair
from rainbows within!

(Free Style)

"The High Road"

Verse I
Upon the page plays dappled moon-kissed light;
aged pen in hand drawn full with lifetime's ink,
awaiting schemes from poets' sanguine plight,
yet full – the parchment ever thirsts for drink.

Verse II
Tho, "Paradox" works up to "Paradigm",
with "Paradise" our hope along the way,
assured we are that rhythm leads to rhyme ...
while wordsmiths pack their verses on a sleigh.

Verse III
Before us waits the high road cloaked 'neath snow.
Let's harness-up the cache and soon depart.
We'll find our dreams, for who's to doubt they're so;
whilst beckons – every kindred poet's heart.

Heroic Couplet
Thus, we'll sing full ... each song of life's spent years,
and spiel our verse by naught but grateful tears.

(English Sonnet)
In homage to our poets' hearts, comes Winter nigh.

ROMANCE

Endless Life ~

The rising sun, cool morning dew,
leaves dancing on soft breeze.
In all the world around lives You;
soft glows your colors' ease.

Slip into slacks 'n sandals, too;
shirtless, I take a walk.
Each taken step a step for two,
our hearts in silent talk.

Stroll we along in loving grace
'til all our cares have flown;
tender the light to match thy face,
your touch ignites my own.

Then, leaning back you pull me down
atop ~ between your thighs,
the universe whirling around,
all life's shared in our eyes.

Beneath their treetop homes we lie,
God's birds and creatures play.
Above it all, a clear blue sky ...
we have our blissful way.

Romance

Our kisses gift all we've longed for,
each breath a lifetime's sigh,
as fauna silently adore ~
in harmony our cry.

In sweet accord they sing along,
we rest there wrapped-up tight,
while thrum two souls life's endless song,
clinging with all our might.

In us, all time has ceased to turn,
the world and all its strife;
never more deep will passions burn,
You are my endless life ~

———~**~———————————————————

(Ballad)

Gifting Stars~~~~~*

Kiss me, you'll see heavenly stars ~
love me, and I'll share them to you.
We'll swing from Jupiter to Mars,
soaring the galaxy all through.

I'll write, "I love you!" 'cross the skies,
circle around the honey moon;
then, sprinkle stardust in your eyes ...
on Venus we'll be dancing soon.

We'll slide down moonbeams soft aglow,
glide clear across the Milky Way.
it's then, My Darling, we'll both know,
wrapped in love's arms we'll always stay.

Heavenly songs, soft-strummed guitars,
across the universe, us two.
Kiss me and you will see bright stars ...
Don't leave ~ I'll gift them all to you.

(Quatrains)

~ In that Moment ~

The last thing on my lips, a prayer for Thee,
sent just before my eyes close for the night,
that every sweet wish in your dreams soar free ...
caressing deep with flowing, warm delight.

Soon, drifting-off, a gentle whisper heard,
as though the universe embraced my soul,
and from afar there came a wondrous word ...
'twas spake in such a way my heart it stole.

A simple word that beckoned that I "Come!"
It was not harsh nor uttered in demand;
yet, as a breath from life's deep primal thrum,
as though you'd laid your heartbeat in my hand.

Then, in that moment ... inside, lit a flame;
your heart and mine became ~ one and the same.

(English Sonnet)

~ Let's do it all again! ~
_____~~**~~_____

That life brought us together then
was not a choice we made,
but more the plan from a wise hand
that's never seemed to fade.

We've been together quite awhile,
I know You will agree...
that, all-in-all, life's sweeter now,
'cause love has set us free.

Came hard times, true, to challenge us;
yet, love has conquered all,
each time with victory's sweet prize ~
deeper in-love we'd fall.

We've many times sat wondering
what's life for us in store,
praising our stars for all we have,
love gifts us even more.

Romance

*Whom could who feels what all we do
not yearn a deeper bite,
when each delicious taste we take
flavors our world just right?*

*Dancing tears from laughter derived,
fall sad when wrought by pain;
but, oh my dear, sweet lover dear,
let's do it all again!*

———————~~**~~———————

(Ballad)

Memory's Gifts

With morning tea, wafts a spell
my wandering mind must tell,
of fairer moments shared along the way.

Crystal pond, wave cattails tall,
of life's joys, I've known most all;
yet, to a sunny smile does mem'ry stray.

'Tis recalled...sweet, tender lips,
emerald eyes, red wine sips
that always led us into passion's play.

Soft aglow...like gleaming gold
life's tenderest gifts unfold;
in every sip I taste your sweet bouquet.

(Primetime)

My Prayer~*

I knelt upon my knees last night
to thank You for your love,
and asked that everyone might know
such blessings from above.
That they, too, walk down flowered lanes
that wend through lea and glen,
beside the brook with sparkling glints
and know such joy within.
Please keep, dear forest, safe our path
we strolled, lost-in love's dreams;
in rhythm, two hearts beat as one
through sprays of bright sunbeams.
Let every breeze and bird with song
rejoice and love be known,
like this of ours, by all the world,
until all fears have flown.
Take love's pure mantle, spread it wide
o'er land and every sea,
that each one's heart and soul embrace
with spirits soaring free.
Arising to slip into bed
came gentle, tender care,
when softest breath felt brush my lips ~
I knew you'd shared my prayer.

(Ballad)

One Desert Night ~

One cool, dark night, bright stars above ...
bloom cactus flow'rs o'er moonlit sand.
Soft, soothing, cooing desert dove,
quiet descends 'cross starlit land.

Bloom cactus flow'rs o'er moonlit sand;
coyote's howls, I'm lonesome, too.
Quiet descends 'cross starlit land;
'neath tall saguaro, dreams ensue.

Coyotes' howls, I'm lonesome, too;
behind my eyes your face takes shape.
'Neath tall saguaro, dreams ensue;
in harmony ~ this world escape.

Behind my eyes your face takes shape;
lips soft like down caress my soul.
In harmony ~ this world escape,
while making-love, flow one and whole.

Lips soft like down caress my soul;
soft, soothing, coos the desert dove ...
while making-love, flow one and whole,
one cool, dark night, bright stars above.

(Pantoum)

OUR PSALMS

In placid silence of darkness I write ...
songs weeping from my hungered yearning soul,
that sing unto me of slow, fading light ...
recalling moments lonely heartaches stole.

When days were young and time was all I had,
I'd thought each morrow was a promised gift;
each one brought something new, but always sad;
and, all my seasons passed-on much too swift.

Seeped o'er, a mist of unrelenting gloom,
each dream a rose that died upon its vine.
A sudden chill crept in, cold as a tomb;
never those days were sweet, like sun-kissed wine.

'Twas then thrummed in my heart a melody;
swiftly and sweet, throughout the soul it flowed
as tho soft wings of angels swept me free ...
all darkness lifted, soft my being glowed.

Each moment, I now worship it in joy ...
cast, too, away all sorrows 'pon the wind.
These golden gifts from You I did employ,
to mantle o'er ache's grip for burdens' end.

Behind the Smile!

I'll sip more slowly moments from time's well,
savor heady hours from mem'ries past;
seek how to smile and dance inside your spell,
drinking my fill of You and love ~ at last!

When wakes each golden sunrise, you're the gifts
that sing life into me from endless ages ...
whilst pens spill stardust ink in sparkling drifts
of psalms – inscribed upon our poems' pages.

———————————~**~———————————

(Ballad)

~ Out There ~

I want to touch the stars at night,
to gather them around me tight,
to dream of us when stars shine bright,
and wish You here with all my might.

Then, if I can and if I do
make each and every wish come true,
the colors bright turn us into
a universe of Me and You.

We'll spread our arms on high alar,
to touch each planet, every star,
slide down soft moonbeams from afar;
entwined, two hearts of cinnabar.

O' take my hand and feel the flow,
there's nothing purer to bestow,
embrace me now, set us aglow,
out there ~ where only dreamers go.

(Quatrains in Monorhyme)

Sealed With A Kiss

Into my heart your words were sent,
pure passions flowing from your core,
that I receive your full consent
to know you'll love me evermore.

The atmosphere ... vibrant, aglow,
and every star above me winks,
because with You I'll always know
just what it is that your heart thinks.

Sure, time or two I've sat in thought,
"Now, I wonder what she's feeling?"
but then I'd laugh when I was caught ...
such uncertainty revealing,

just how silly I was to doubt
or let myself be insecure;
then, reach and pull your poems out
to read your words that reassure.

Into my arms, upon your breasts,
I feel your presence make us one;
For, thereon Thou my head doth rest,
and all resistance comes undone.

Romance

No one but You can touch my all,
my heart tells me that this is true.
as soft, sweet whispers I hear call ~
each one a warm, wet kiss from You.

The sparrow gazing, tilts its head,
in wonder at my soul's soft song,
and chirping with its wings outspread,
in harmony ~ sings right along.

Behind closed eyes ~ You come to me,
imbuing deeply every place;
as with each breath, soar spirits free,
like roses' scent, your sweet embrace.

Those days and nights of yearning pain,
all now replaced in loving bliss,
when in a moment's sweet refrain ...
two lovers' vows ~ sealed with a kiss*

———————~**~———————————

(Ballad)

~ She loves me, too ~

She pled, "Please, write me no more songs,
give them to someone else;
for, all they do is gather dust
and rot there on my shelf."

Tho, it hurt deep to hear her words,
I knew just what they meant;
'twas understood the feelings hid
her now cold heart had sent.

Poems I write that she'll ne'er read ...
I share them now with all;
this heart of mine can't still it's voice,
it yet hears her love's call.

I know she will deny I've heard
those words flow from her heart,
but well I know that voice so sweet
that touched me from the start,

and on each night my head lies down,
a prayer forms in my soul,
and swear I do she answers true,
"I love you deep and whole."

May be but hope-filled love lives on,
    when untrue love should die,
but when I hear the wind-chime's sing,
    my lonely dreams yet sigh.

There is no doubt she's here with me,
a smile spreads through and through ...
then, when my world turns colors bright,
I know ~ She loves me, too ~

———————————~**~———————————

(Ballad)

Springtime's Warm Embrace ~

Soft through low passes breezes warmly blow,
and everywhere bright flowers start to bloom;
pure melting snow sends rivulets a'flow,
as tender shoots end Winter's long, hard gloom.

Tall elder, spruce, and lodgepole kiss the sky,
amidst high boughs the eagle build its home,
across the meadowlands they hunt and fly ...
where elk and whitetail birth their young and roam.

Bright scarlet trumpets set the fields aflame,
and thaws last vestiges of winter snows.
It's then my heart and soul calls out your name,
with tender whispered touches love bestows.

When comes the signs of springtime's warm embrace ~
it's then I'll feel your sweet breath on my face.

(English Sonnet)

LIFE

Come 'N Share

When peeks the morning sun to greet our eyes,
inspired hearts dance into day's luring thrill,
each stretch and yawn, the spirit's hopes arise;
for, 'tis the moment last night's dreams fulfill.

O' Walnut, spread your branches wide and tall.
Such glory is the melody that sings
amidst your limbs before their leaves all fall,
as sparrows witness squirr'ls' meanderings.

Off in the distance wails a train's low moan,
cicadas saw a tune they know so well;
it's by this way we know we're not alone,
for we've been cast a part in Life's great spell.

Upon bare knees I kneel in grateful prayer,
inviting all my friends to come 'n share.

(English Sonnet)

Down on the Farm

Sunrise, warming the heart, tugs at my soul,
peeks over yon hills to make the day whole.

Soft grass bejeweled by dew, each daffodil ~
bluebird singin' on the old windowsill.

Out thar 'cross the meadows, soft church bells ring,
"G'mornin', Ya'll!" Ma's sweet voice I hear sing.

Biscuits are steamin', hot crisp bacon, too,
Johnny, Melinda, 'n Little Sis Sue,

Brother Robbie ... homemade butter 'n jam,
eggs over-easy, a fried slice of yam!"

His truck's windin' up the road by the lake,
"Come on, Pa, don't be late – for goodness sake!

We're hungry as horses rarin' to go;
aw, come on now, Pa, quit driven' so slow!"

After eatin' read the Sunday funnies,
the paper ya bought from saved-up monies.

Then, we all spiff-up in our Sunday best,
to hear young Preacher Keith sermon with zest.

Melinda says he's handsome and gallant,
and Momma thinks he's loaded with talent.

Pa likes him 'cause he's one fine kinda man;
our country church doin' best as it can.

Behind the Smile!

*The kids group together for Sunday School,
where Deacon Garth teaches The Golden Rule.*

*Melinda, she fawns, 'cause he's handsome, too,
the teens squirm a'waitin' till it's all through;*

*so, in the lake they can all take a swim,
climb the big oak tree and dive from its limb.*

*There hangs a rope tied, to an old wornout tire;
they swing to and fro, higher 'n higher.*

*Johnny, the rascal, he winks at the girls,
they blush and giggle, while twirling their curls.*

*Grown folk a'watchin' there's no hanky-pank,
the young kids are always pullin' a prank.*

*When caught they're assigned to cranking' the churn,
each (one at a time) is taking their turn.*

*The picnic tables laid-out with a feast ...
everyone's appetite by now's increased.*

*Dessert is sweet ice cream all the kids churned,
each filled and fulfilled before they've adjourned.*

*I'll never forget life down on the farm,
or my Momma's face and her graceful charm.*

*These beautiful scenes I gaze on with love,
beholding dearly ... from here up above.*

(Rhyming Couplets)

~//~DUSTY DIRT ROAD~//~
~ just a kid ~

—//—

Bucket and a well
log-windlass crank-n-rope,
Cool water soothe my face
sun, warm-glory fill my hope.

Out into the woods
so loose and fancy-free,
Flyin' down the old rabbit trail
swimmin' hole awaitin' on me.

Red, Georgia clay so fine
color to these young bare feet,
Isenglass pit reflectin' my joy
mica in a thin clear crystal sheet.

Snap outta loose bib-overalls
nothing on anyway underneath,
Climb into twisted limbs so high
pool below a sparkln' rippled-wreath.

Behind the Smile!

Hawk eyes under blue sky reels
watch frolicky squirrels at play,
Deer witness all from yon bank
happiness please don't go astray.

Supine upon that boulder so warm
Indian signs from days gone yore,
Climb again that curled-limb route
swan dive into that mirror once more.

Whistle a tune, skip ta ma lou
backwards run with no weary-heart load,
Cartwheel across the ol' catchin' ditch
blackberry pickin'-n-skippin' again
down
that
ol'
"Dusty Dirt Road"

—//—

(Unmetered Quatrains w/Envoi)

"To go back and be free at peace and ease ... one with nature alive ... what I'd give as a man if I could again be oh so innocent ~ ah, for but a day!"

I am a Man, and I am Free!
just another day in the big city...

I stir when sunrise tips its golden cup,
to spill its light upon the newfound day;
with sleepy eyes I wake and then stand up
on newfound legs to face life's frantic fray.
"Yesss, bring it onnnn!" I yawn out on the world,
while stretching wide and tall, with arms unfurled.
It's now begins those tasks and labors new,
until my final days on earth are through.
The man I will become depends on me.
I've said so many times, and know it's true
these words, "I am a man, and I am free!"

The wake-up shower calls – a nice, close shave...
thick, comfy socks lie waiting in their draw'r.
Which shirt to wear today, shall I be brave,
or be the same dependable old bore?
Familiar denim jacket fits just right;
it's not too loose a fit, nor is it tight.
A man has got to wear his good ol' jeans,
to show 'em all just what it is he means,
and who it is he's proudly meant to be...
while climbing high up on his big machines
to say, "I am a man, and I am free!"

My hard hat I flipped on and slammed the door...
outside, the old red truck awaits my hand,
to turn the key and start it up once more.
Today will be hard work, I understand,
but fighting traffic is my present goal;
I shift into first gear and let 'er roll.
Now, out onto the road upon my way,
I'm off again to earn my daily pay,
that takes care of my loving family.
Another buck, it's only one more day;
oh yes, "I am a man, and I am free!"

I'm here, if I can only find a place
to park this sweet old honey of a truck,
I'll not be late again and in disgrace;
so, "Aye, I need to have a bit of luck!
Ah, there's a spot, I'm going to pull right in,
then start the day the way it should've been."
"What is it now?" I hear an angry shout,
"You're in my space, now you get the hell out!"
"What's that? Damned if I will!" yelled out of me.
"Hah! I'm the big man on this job, you clout!"
Hear me, "I am a man, and I am free!"

He taunted, "I don't give a big, fat fig!
I've always been the Big Man all my life.
Into that space of mine I'll park this rig!
Get out, or taste the sharp edge my knife!"
"I'm just not in a mood for you today,
to hear your silly guff or with you play;
so, my advice is for you to desist;
or, THAT knife up in your ugly ass I'll twist!"
His face turned red, but it was not in glee;
while offering to give him my big fist,
I yelled, "I am a man, and I am free!"

I should've known right then 'twas not my day,
when I arose and smiled with thoughts of pay.
Life never seems, for me, to turn out right.
Now, I'm confronted by this silly fight.
Why can't this dumb ass just come-to and see?
Ohhhh, NO! I've been stabbed deep, my life's in flight!"
At last, "I am a Man ... and, I am FREE ~"

(Chant Royal)

LIFE'S SONG

Beneath grayed cloak the evergreens reach high
   to drink from air, their needles weighted full.
Limbs supple, softer than an unborn sigh,
   below a mist, give way to Nature's pull.

At night, soft whispers you may nigh hear of;
   oh, do not fear and turn to run from such;
for, only 'tis the kiss of winds above,
   in chilling flight – upon life's lips, its touch.

Amidst those mists and shadows lies a shrine
   of vine-made arbors ... gravestones for the dead.
An angel stands its guard, by Death's design,
   that peaceful comfort's wrought, when life has fled.

Should thou soar high between that angel's wings,
hold tight with faith; then, hear the song life sings.

(English Sonnet)

♪ LIFE'S SWEET MUSIC ♫

─────────────~**~─────────────

♪

When music plays,
my mind ~ it sways
to heaven's beat on earth.
Feet start tapping,
hands start clapping,
life's rhythm's given birth.♮

♩

Melody sings,
such joy it brings,
while all about's a-spin.
I must let go,
dance to 'n fro ...
life's beat thrums deep within.♭

♫

I hear the sound
that's coming down,
it grabs and won't release;
so, what's to do
but play it through
'til life's encore brings peace.♯

♪

─────────────~**~─────────────

(Quickie)

"MARRIAGE"
(as if anyone knows)

GOOD
marriage
is a union of two forgivers.

SUCCESSFUL
marriage
means falling in love many times,

ALWAYS,
with the same person.

(Free Verse)

Moving-time ...

'Twas once our hearts upon the parchment danced,
in jubilee and joy our voices rang;
in tenderness and love, how we romanced,
and every song that could be sung ~ we sang.

Now, tomes of poems are tightly stowed away,
t'ward their new homes ... wherever that may be,
and onward rush we all in disarray,
like lemurs headed for some unknown sea.

O' memories embrace me one last time,
in comfort for the years we shan't reclaim;
but, shed no tears to recompensing rhyme ...
nor, lack of knowing who or what to blame.

'Tis destiny that leads us into fate;
if truth be known, now ... I can barely wait.

(English Sonnet)

Poor man's lullaby ~

Here I am, where I've come to be ...
while, a'way back over yonder,
a past so harsh then ... never free,
life's memories sadly wander.

He, whom I was / now've grown into,
scantly resemble each other.
That which I've been is known by few;
ghetto brothers, I watched smother.

Life came too hard, out of control ...
each step we took was two steps back;
what few coins earned were quickly stole.
Adults? Each one was far too slack.

The path we trod was once their path,
'twas destined that which came before,
that every child would reap the wrath ...
seemed-like, there was nothing more.

Life's ladder short ... a dead-end street,
so many mothers sit and cry;
now, looking back, years gone too fleet,
my song's a poor man's lullaby!

(Quatrains in 8-Count)

STREETS OF HOUSTON

I.

There was a woman struggling on her own,
who birthed one night a son with eyes sky blue.
His hair was soft and gleamed a golden tone,
on her soft lips a smile ~ in her heart too.

His sleeper PJs had a button flap,
with booties soft that kept young toes so warmed,
and comfort of a loving mother's lap...
unto her breast his mouth was gently formed.

Came toys and playthings a young boy adores
that one day helps to make the man he'll be ...
all kept with pride, stacked neatly into draw'rs;
aligned, just like a toy-land's bright marquee.

And so it was, began this toddler's life;
with his sweet mother, an abandoned wife.

II.
With his sweet mother, an abandoned wife,
his years progressed until a boy emerged.
The ghetto streets were mean that formed his life,
where future plans from worldly woes converged

and taught such lessons all young men should learn;
of how to walk through fear, yet fear no one;
to fight a better fistfight with each turn,
then be the fastest to escape and run.

Was learned man's law, and hard laws from the street,
as each one to its own was justice born,
and where the dreams of love and life ne'er meet,
except that justice was revenge so sworn.

Morality, a lesson mothers taught...
in those mean streets there are no morals wrought.

III.

In those mean streets there are no morals wrought,
    lest save the ones that twist and snare the soul.
It's sad that boys and girls become distraught
    before their life allows them to be whole.

There were no freeways built yet in those days;
    though, were those certain aspects – looking back,
    which made the world, by far, a better place;
    we used no dope and never heard of crack.

The doors were kept unlocked…kids came and went,
    and never was there fear from an adult
    of stepping out of line in sharp extent;
because, they knew with kids, the sharp result

    could be a fatal dose of recompense…
    not one adult adopted lack of sense.

IV.
Not one adult adopted lack of sense;
tho, we were loners, we could act as one,
and not one would, commit such an offense
that made their life and world come all undone.

It's in this way the unsure balance kept
what made survival possible at all;
for, though, the many children I've known wept,
there's no revenge unsettled, I recall.

Thus, is such justice in my ghetto home,
and though I'd change no single day for me,
I'm glad the man in me set out to roam.
From all I've learned I'd set the young ones free,

but they're too locked-in by the hands of fate.
Bless all of them before it is too late.

V.

Bless all of them before it is too late.
I've done most all that I can think to do,
but never shall I stop or hesitate
in giving everything while I pursue

a better way to reach and inspire hope,
'til every girl and boy has heard my prayers,
and every mother that's been left to cope
knows that there's someone left who really cares.

Sure, this I know, is trite and filled with dread,
that seldom anyone considers them;
for, I have all too often heard it said
lost kids are better left to serve life's whim.

When I hear this, my heart begins to weep...
I know the walls they'll have to climb are steep.

VI.

I know the walls they'll have to climb are steep,
    and odds are but a few survive their fall;
one thing I know for sure is they must keep
    on clinging to the ladder, one and all.

Come on, each one, up to the top ascend...
then, proud and tall, descend the other side!
What choices left them, other than pretend,
    and sink into the shadow's deep deride.

Oh, please, hear well and learn with hopeful mind;
    then, promise to shed veils of dark dismay.
Remember, those who persevered and find,
    also, for you there always is a way.

I know the odds seem you will fall and lose...
if you don't try, you'll have no chance to choose.

VII.

If you don't try, you'll have no chance to choose;
sit idle by, upon your doubtful hands,
still moping, simmer in your self-stirred stews..
surrender NOT to poverty's demands!

So many from my youth have passed along,
and many more live in a prison cell.
I tell you now to sing a diff'rent song,
or ever life will be a living hell.

No better I'm than any of you there;
although, I may be better off, it's true...
it's all because, I've learned how to prepare,
and high above that wall to life I flew.

When you see her, tell her she's not alone...
there "was" a woman struggling on her own!

(Crown of Sonnets)

Behind the Smile!

(Streets Of Houston)
Author's Comments:
A few noted individuals that made it out of
Houston's Northside Ghettos

Red Adair...Oilwell Firefighter, Roger Clemens...Baseball Player
Rodney Crowell...Country Singer, Jimmy Demaret...Pro Golfer
George Foreman...Boxer, A.J. Foyt...Race Car Driver
Walter Cronkite...Broadcast Journalist, Geto Boys...Rap Group Lisa Hartman...Actress, Howard Hughes...Oil Entrepreneur
Richard Jenkins...Poet, Karate Fighter/Teacher, Entrepreneur
Beyoncé Knowles...Pop Singer, John Osteen...Pastor
Barbara Mandrell...Country Singer, Jaclyn Smith...Actress
Jerry Newberry...Country Singer, Patrick Swayze...Actor
Mickey Leland...Anti-Poverty Activist, Barbara Jordan...Politician
David Koresh...Infamous Cult Leader, Mark Calaway...Wrestler
Annette O'Toole...Actress, Phylicia Rashad...Actress
Kenny Rogers...Country Singer, B.J. Thomas...Pop Singer
Tommy Tune...Actor, JoBeth Williams...Actress

~ Sweet, Youthful Years

When we were children, growing-up,
no puddle ever went un-stomped,
no stray was left without a home,
and morn' till dark we laughed 'n romped.

Lightnin' bugs blink soft in a jar,
butterflies pinned neat to a board;
held on by a clothespin, each cape ...
across skies, like Superman soared.

No tree worth its climbing unclimbed,
from hickory-twigs slingshots were made,
stung hard, Chinaberries, just right;
such memories never will fade.

Cardboard stands ~ nickel lemonade,
yards were cut for merely a buck.
Lost bottles were quickly redeemed,
Saturday morn movies, potluck!

Without chain-guards, fender-less bikes
and handlebars turned upside-down.
Right pant's leg rolled-up, playing cards
on spokes made a motorbike sound.

Behind the Smile!

*Keds for kids and patches on jeans,
sandlot football was the best game...
played 'til we dropped, sleeping like logs,
ne'er again will times be the same.*

*When we were children, growing-up
we would say, "Yes, Ma'am and yes, Sir!"
got quiet when we were told to,
and dared not sass back – that's for sure.*

*Dad worked all day, Mom stayed at home,
made cookies, and kissed 'way our pain.
Doors never were locked, nor the cars.
If I could, I'd live it again.*

*Come on, you kids, shut down the screens;
they'll wait ... not so, innocent cares.
Enjoy being a child (while you can),
wasting no more ~ sweet youthful years.*

(Quatrains in 8-Count)
Partly true, but mostly an ideal only dreamed of.

TEXAS WILDFIRES

Higher! Higher roars God's great fire ...
behind, naught's left but ashen pyre!
The winds blew strong for far too long;
flames fed where they did not belong.

Sparks flew through trees on angry breeze,
to rid the land of all that please ...
consumed what may all in the way ...
nothing but death's left in its fray.

"Thou hath betrayed," the masses prayed,
"why hard's Thy hand upon us laid?
God, we deride!" some people cried,
while others kept Him by their side.

No answer came from He they blame,
'til all fell lost to wretched flame.
Gone – flora green, fauna unseen,
forests they roamed and grew pristine;

It seems a shame to take in vain
that which was gained by seed and rain;
yet, Nature knows nor cares what grows,
only by dying – life bestows.

Behind the Smile!

Aye, hear His voice in pow'r rejoice,
"E'er "I" shall always give thee choice;
and, how ye choose, love, or abuse
decides if thou're to win or lose.

So, heed The Word, let it be heard;
embrace what's pure and not absurd!
Build not upon to soon be gone;
build faith anew with each new dawn.

Rise thee to stand upon My hand,
to see beyond thy homes and land.
When storm and fire raze thine empire ...
then, t'ward yon higher realm aspire."

(Fours 'n Eights)

~ The Joys In Life ~

What more could man want
than life never daunt,
or bring challenge he can't ever win?
To have such a plan,
makes a happy man
to have learned from the places he's been.

The real joys in life
are born from sheer strife;
the kind that tests from best in us all.
It's better to know
what helps us all grow,
that picks us up whenever we fall.

So, say your prayers well;
one never can tell
when they'll be answered in measures full.
Reach out with deep hope,
when trying to cope
with all the tasks upon us that pull;

and, it is no joke
that we should invoke
everything that's been granted our way.
"What better" I ask,
"is finer the task...
than to harvest joys sown from each day?"

(Chardelle)

Three kinds of kids ...

When we were children,
growing-up was
the last thing
on our minds.

Where,
was there room
for anything, other than ...
laughter that made our tummies ache,
our sides feel like splitting
that made jaws sore,
things that filled our souls
with more youthful love,
as was befitting?

Even though,
we had no way of knowing
what love really was;
and, too...
being truthful,
I'm still not all that sure
I do.

Counting stars,
fireflies caught in jars,
drinking water from a well,
the whole wide world was swell.

Life

When we were children,
growing-up
we did not know ...
that other children had no homes,
that joy for them was a piece of bread,
there was no place to lie their head,
winters cold and summers long,
crying was their only song.

Had we known
what would we do ...
would we go and be a friend,
swear a vow until the end,
our toys to them send?

Well,
now I'm grown,
or so they say ...
never have I found a way
for sharing all of this –
the love
I've always had.

When we were children,
growing-up,
I was called,

"That boy who's bad!"

(Free Style)

'Til all life ends...

A seed-rich earth and rain warmed by the sun,
each blade of grass a'dance in wind's soft sigh,
as waking flowers smile – 'til day is done...
the bliss-filled kiss, tears gentle lovers cry,
soft, golden morning rays that bless all life
with colours, that our eyes and souls might know
such joys to make it worth our toil and strife.
It is from these (and endless more) we grow,
and each becomes the being that we are;
yet, as I gaze out on the world each day,
when nighttime falls beneath each dazzling star,
it never ceases to amaze the way
in which we love, and how our love transcends,
like wind and rain and sun – 'Til all life ends...

(English Sonnet)

LOVE

–LOVE–

...to all its seekers...

Love shall seek not....
but for its own satisfaction;
nor, will it be easily
swayed from its course.

It cannot....
be captured
and will not be controlled
by anything other than love, itself.

For....
Love is sufficient unto Love,
and can be known only
to itself.

Nothing known can destroy genuine Love.

"There is no single answer to the question
of what love really is,
but "this" I have found it is to me ~
perhaps, now, to you!"

(Free Verse)

~ Attuned to Love ~

How pure these thoughts through our minds flow;
for, we're attuned to love.
Warm passions of our tender ways
conform us hand and glove.

Each star a'glint in stratosphere,
the pale and wat'ry moon...
reflect in each 'n every dream,
sweet melodies we croon.

Soft rhythms dance within the heart
no one save us can hear.
We're promised an eternity
for all that we hold dear.

All this 'n more, our bonds embrace
sweet blessings from above,
created and reflected by
this life we share in-love.

(Ballad w/Envoi)

Autumn and You

I miss You, Darling, and love You so much,
your angelic face, your soft, warming touch.

It's Early Autumn, the leaves are still green;
hues of your eyes ~ most beautiful I've seen.

Soon, all will turn golden, like your soft hair ...
with a blessing ~ I'll see You everywhere.

Too, a myriad of colors galore,
like You, mysteries of wonders in store.

I'll turn my collar up from the cold chill,
keep warm our dreams for that day to be still.

Seasons of ours, they come and they go ...
again, it's Autumn ~ I still love You so.

(Rhyming Couplets)

~ How you'll know I Love You ~

You'll know I love you from the gentle rain
that falls across the land to grace each leaf,
beside you in your dreams where I have lain,
each touch of me that's gently soothed your grief.

As crowning mists embrace yon mountain's crest,
glows o'er the valley's moors, morn's golden hue;
each yellow rose that blooms you will be blessed,
reflecting in your own ~ my eyes so blue.

When evening's moon glows quietly 'cross the land
stand by your window, then you'll hear my name,
when like a warming breath upon your hand
your ear will feel my whisper light the flame.

So, think not ever from thee I'll be led ...
for, fate's two loving hearts ~ forever wed.

Behind the Smile!

~————————~.•.~————————~

You'll know I love you when you're anywhere
life's treasures strike your mind as brightly-full;
when then, you close your eyes and I am there,
you'll feel my golden touch on your heart's pull.

—~.•.~—

When finches build their nests you'll ponder me,
as wind-chimes play soft melodies you'll know,
that all the world's a place where I will be ...
deep in your swelling breast emotions grow.

—~.•.~—

While tender tears e'er grateful well and fall,
by each you'll know within your soul I soar.
In you my breath's forever, after-all ...
with this dwells proof of Us forevermore.

—~.•.~—

Throughout your moments, always I'll imbue.
By these and more ~ you'll know how I love You.

~————————~.•§•.~————————~

(Sonnet Doublet)

Lemon Avenue, Flowers and You

As I walked along Lemon Avenue,
I thought of you and love,
and smelled the sweet scent of flowers in bloom.

Lee Park, down by Turtle Creek,
is a lovely place for any free-faring valiant
to ponder all the voyages of yesterday,
but, the beauty to me is now
and the closeness of you it seems to bring,
with its solitude and soft, green grass.

I watched a cloud and a plane,
and, the leaves became your emerald eyes,
the wind your golden hair softly caressing my face,
and the carrier of our gentle embraces.

Can one love so completely
as to exchange in a moment,
the true warmth of a kiss
with its irreplaceable memory?

Seclusion from the world is my goal,
until time and life give its approval of our love.

I'm so lonesome, I sometimes cry,
while the world around me
is bright and glittering.

I have only to catch a ride
on a passing laugh,
but, none came my way today.

Oh, well...
there are lots of them around
... most anytime.

It's not that I don't appreciate
all the nice and beautiful things around me...
I cherish them so,
and they are important.
It's just that I am so used to
such a higher realm of happiness
than the rest of the world has to offer.

It is the absence of you
that leaves me lonely and empty now ...

Until our time comes,
I'll stroll along Lemon Avenue,
and become lost in the sweet scent of flowers,
and You — "and, I waited for the longest."

(Free Verse)

Love Psalm for My Lover ~

Your breath I felt swirl deep within my soul ...
as touches moved throughout me softly warmed,
the world turned brightly pure, like burnished gold,
as images of You ~ in my heart formed.
Behind closed eyes you danced into my view,
like misty, dancing shadows 'cross the wall.
In pirouetting leaps and bounds You flew ...
'twas then I heard that sweet, familiar call.
"O' come, My Love, into these arms of mine,
embrace this warmth ~ inside mine, pour your own
... that evermore our luscious flows entwine,
eternal seeds our fated life has sown."
The atmosphere then filled with Autumn Rose,
a love psalm only true hearts could compose.

(English Sonnet)

Love's Pendulum

Your breath so warm upon my face,
my blood and heart begin to race,
and every fiber in every place,
my thoughts wander to your sweet grace,
soft breasts greet mine as we embrace,
your lips I'm kissing, just in case.

One never knows what fate might bring,
what songs of joy the soul's voice sing,
for love is such a mercurial thing,
it may be a lifetime, or a night's wild fling,
there is no telling where next it would spring,
we never know how ... love's pendulum will swing.

(Mono-rhymed Verses)

Loving You ~

*Love's glow to light your spark'ling eyes
with wondrous flowers everywhere,
rainbows painted 'cross the skies,
gold, shiny ribbons for your hair,*

*and all sweet joy can ever bring,
a love that never dies,
songs for your tender heart to sing,
a book of poems composed from sighs.*

*Then, as the day moves gently 'long
that all is rightly filled with bliss,
and every call of each bird's song
thrills the heart like love's warm kiss.*

*All these (and more) I wish for You ~
so there will never be a doubt
of what takes place in me all through ...
what loving You is all about.*

(Quatrains in 8-Count)

Making Memories~

With happy heart his old pen spiels its ink
in words that dance and sing upon the page.
Some say that they're most beautiful, they think,
some even say they could become the rage.

With humble bow he knows that he's been blessed;
what's to be said but, "Thank you!" as he blushed.
He's but a simple bard, he has confessed,
who knows, by wondrous love, he has been brushed.

Of all who come to read his poetry,
there is but one who sparks his heartbeats' flame,
and so high on his list of probity
he has been heard to outwardly exclaim,

"Oh, please, My Love, come read my verse to thee ~
in every word's a golden memory."

(English Sonnet)

My darling golden rose ~

_~~**~~_

You know, Sweetheart? I've sat and thought
of all that's good and bad;
of for what purpose it was wrought
I naught but make You sad.

Then, took a closer look at me,
and saw what's to berate;
for all the good I've tried to be,
seems failure is my fate.

I pray each night and all day long
that I might turn to good,
but surely I am meant for wrong;
this now is understood.

If comes an angel such as You,
and still I haven't changed,
although your heart is ever true,
we've now become estranged.

So many chances You have gave
to mend my sorry ways;
many times I've tried to behave,
when You gave me your praise.

Behind the Smile!

I'm still the knave I always was,
that's how I am, it seems.
You've filled my world with joyous buzz;
I've only stained your dreams.

Oh, please, my angel from above,
forgive me for your sake,
that You might dance again and love
a man who won't forsake

the fairest woman of them all,
with heart of gold to give.
Throw me away and do not stall,
there's happiness to live.

Paint me over with colours grey,
remove me from your scene.
Me, replace with flowers each day,
of precious gold and green.

You've served your purpose, setting free
this cold hard heart of mine;
taught me to love, and now I plea,
spit out my bitter wine.

Sincerely, I apologize
for wasting your dear time.
Your luring smile, soft verdant eyes,
our every word of rhyme,

I'll not forget eternity;
once ~ it was yours and mine.
We loved in sweet serenity,
shared passions so divine.

Then, darkness came I thought was cured,
and other sickness deep;
such pain I wreaked, but you endured,
my cost proved much too steep.

There is no flower that can grow,
without its nourishment,
for each and every seed You sew
was one more I had spent.

You tended with your gentle hand
our garden filled with love,
but every tender shoot to stand,
I made dead fodder of.

That which confuses me so much
is what is wrong with me ...
You gift me light from your charmed touch;
yet, still I cannot see.

Yon sun is shining warm and pure,
the mockingbird sings sweet;
when You look down you'll see for sure,
it's me kissing your feet.

Behind the Smile!

Oh, bless the very ground You walk,
I'll always dream of You,
of all our moments shared in talk,
deep romance known by few.

I'll hold no blame and call your name
when spells of darkness smite,
and evermore I'll dream your frame
around me warm and tight.

Just one last prayer before I go:
Please, think of me and smile,
remembering I love You so,
and you loved me awhile.

Alas, I'll ne'er fill your desires;
not now, I might suppose;
still, you'll e'er be ... 'til life expires,
My darling golden rose ~

———————~~**~~———————

(Ballad)

~ Nighttime Reverie ~

As softly I lay down my head to rest,
a voice I'd longed to hear spake to my soul,
"Outside, I wait to hold you to my breast,

and down beside the pond we'll take a stroll ...
beneath the stars above, bond one and whole."

'Twas in that moment, shined the brightest light
into my heart – and love was ours that night.

(Rime Royal)

~.˜•'˜Pink Carnations, You & Love˜'•˜.~
~ from my woman's, my flower's perspective ~

~.˜•'˜§˜'•˜.~

Vases, pristinely-white and pure
stand regally within each room,
Pink carnations, adorning each
all to dispel life's direst gloom.

~.~•'~~'•~.~

Petals oh, softly, so tenderly folded
one upon another soft as sea foam,
Aromas sweet as finest, aged wine
waft sublime throughout my home.

~.~•'~~'•~.~

White gypsophila of starry-white
bless those petals pink and sweet,
As I dance, I twirl in gayest glory
upon my feather-light lover's feet.

~.~•'~~'•~.~

Sunbeams steal 'cross ardent floor
to climb legs crafted oh ~ so fine,
To fall upon those heavenly petals;
aglow, this spirited heart of mine.

~.~•'~~'•~.~

..~•'~~'•~.._

I dream of days to come with you
your tides broach upon my shore,
Arm and arm ~ to glide and swing
for a day, a life dear, forevermore.

..~•'~~'•~.._

These pink lovely petals, soft and fine
living moments within my every day,
Like pink carnations and baby's breath
loving You, so beautiful in every way.

..~•'~~'•~.._

Now, I know why God gave them to me
as I arise and glow like the sun each day,
That I'll love and keep you for all my life;
for Pink Carnations, You & Love, I pray.

..~•'~§~'•~.._

.

•

*

(Unmetered Quatrains)

Soft tear ~

I want you to truly know...
oh, My Sweet Beloved Dear,
just how much I need you so
to know gently this soft tear.
No coldest tear for sorrows;
nor, of dreams passed yesterday,
but all of our tomorrows
life's warm winds to send our way.
Kind, soft tear of joyful glee,
none 'cept those in-love can feel,
as it rolls down tenderly
'tween two cheeks a bonding seal.
Your bright heart and mine shared pure,
bound forever ~ love's fate sure.

(Ameri-Sonnet)

~ Through Love ~

'Twas that moment two souls touched they knew;
twin hearts sang, then danced to sweet refrain.
Oh, blest be pain attuned to love,
eternity hath bound thy fate
and freed!
Glory found...heretofore known by few;
life breathed-in, like purest, gentle rain
that whispers joy with every drop,
to renew hope – ingratiate
each need.

Broad oceans deep ... vast lands ... mountains tall,
quelled nor severed what God's plan had made.
When stars aligned, shined down His light...
each prayer knelt and prayed was heard
above.
Heeded, true twin hearts...answered, their call;
once dark, now their colours never fade,
but cast a lasting memory...
two, ordained one – beyond mere word,

through love ~

(Brady's Touch)

___...~·~You Are My Seasons~·~...___

A road so long it does not stop;
the sky so high and blue.
The world is spinning like a top;
my heart beats fast for you.

It's there in every revolution,
the seasons that you are.
On each loop around the sun,
for you I'll hang a star.

In Springtime, you're each bud begun;
Autumn, all colors that we see.
When Summer comes, life's giving sun;
in Winter, you'll be warming me.

As all the seasons come and go,
to me, you will remain the same.
Eternally, I'll love you so;
you'll always be my inner-flame.

Until, at last, my time is here,
I'll know no moment in regret;
it's so, my darling, have no fear,
in You, Sweet Love, all seasons set.

(Unmetered Quatrains)

When, with love ~

There's ne'er a frown,
when new-plowed ground
births early crops a start.
Tools now laid down,
we're homeward bound
t'ward hearth with grateful heart.

Warming delight,
fireplace lit bright,
in prayer for grace we kneel;
keep us held tight
throughout the night,
give thanks for our fine meal.

Faces aglow
from all we'll sow:
Love holds no reproaches.
Now's time to show,
gift, and bestow...
gloaming fast approaches.

Behind the Smile!

Soon, will the night
from day take flight,
heads weary laid to rest.
It's then despite,
resist and fight,
with sleep, each one, we're blest.

Comes quick the dawn,
a sleepy yawn...
fresh, new day for giving;
until we're gone,
thus life goes on...
when, with love ~ we're living.

―――――――~**~―――――――

(Fours 'n Sixes)

EMOTION

What Would Life Be ~

Strolling 'round the pond this morn,
lost in loving thoughts of You ...
in ways, these times, I often do.

Breezes, whispered soft your name,
the sun so warm, I felt you there ...
watched, frogs 'n turtles everywhere.

Dragonfly perched on a cattail frond,
rainbow colors gleamed in its wings;
dearest songs, Mockingbird sings.

It seems the world (smiling with me)
feels as one, with my heartbeat;
upon my own, your lips so sweet.

Unto my soul, your lush kiss spoke,
these thoughts of yours were heard,
"Oh, My Man, hear every word ...

though, life has pulled us far apart,
never, Dear One, shall I forget
all we've shared, since first we met ...

Emotion

nor, every night you've come to me,
every day, in all my tasks ...
always love me, is all I ask!"

Somehow, all trials then swept away,
I felt your warm, tender embrace,
what would life be ~ without your grace!

(Free Style)

when You take the New Roads

———————————~**~———————————

Upon that day You take the new roads there,
be ever mindful of the ways You choose;
remember, too, the ones You leave still care,
that all their hearts and souls ~ you'll never lose.

The road ahead may seem a brighter way,
the visions far – You feel a longing lure,
and everywhere You look a bright, new day;
then, looking back you'll see naught but a blur.

A sort of wavy imagery that fades,
of faces you once knew that smile no more ...
where colours once, now grey and shadowed shades,
as memory becomes a closing door.

Yet, so much more (unknown) is calling now,
and all you've known seems useless now somehow.

———————~**~———————

We'll miss your tender love and gentle hand,
that always knew the touch and words to say,
whenever needed ~ your sweet, special brand
to warm cold dark and sweep the clouds away.

With You, be sure to take all that you'll need;
You know, those little things that were the best ...
like poems of love and promises decreed,
each tender heartbeat made within our breasts.

Aye, heed the road ahead – it's luring call;
and, tarry not lest roads ahead fade, too.
As all you leave here far behind grows small,
remember, Dear ~ I'll always wait for You.

Tho, those new roads may take You far away,
you'll always be my first breath ~ every day.

(English Sonnet Doublet)

Wildflowers ~

Oft' slow I'll pass by the Olde Flower Shop,
adore each delightful bouquet,
considering you'd most surely love one,
but I lack the coinage to pay.

Hang then my head low in sorrowful shame,
strolling sadly on down the road ...
knowing how I have once more let you down,
and it's not so easy a load.

Money troves in the bank nor great riches,
not likely I'll own very much;
yet, all I have to give is yours, my love ...
I'm not very handsome, as such.

My eyes dimmer, too ... tho, still just as blue;
this old heart beats warmly and strong,
while all the time, my thought's dwelling on You,
I know they're there ~ where they belong.

I dream of being your deserving man,
days in-love you'll smile upon me;
all the world alive in its lovely glow,
my spirit soars higher and free.

There 'long the roadside...hopeful, they beckon,
their colours so vividly strong,
in the breeze, lovely wildflowers dancing;
like You ~ in my heart they belong.

There are so many, they beg to be picked,
but I'm not that greedy a guy,
softly caressing the textures of each,
grateful hands agree with the eye.

With bounty held close, aromas so sweet,
no wider smile my face has known.
No vase yet received a lovelier treat,
nor flora from God's fields e'er grown.

It's said I'm not all that much to look at,
my body is not quite as buff;
my hair's thinned-out now, all silver 'n grey,
and my love is never enough.

Yet, I'll strive to be a more worthy man
with money enough that you'll know,
I can afford the most gorgeous bouquet
a man's hand did ever bestow.

Behind the Smile!

*Down on my knees, I'll present it with love,
while begging your forgiveness, too ...
that I'm not up to par – lacking by far,
but I'll try my heart out for You.*

*Meanwhile, darling dear, I hope You can hear
the soft urging beat of my heart.
It's murmuring to You, "Please, accept true,
these Wildflowers ~ as a new start."*

---~**~---

(Quatrains in 10/8 Count)

Woken feelings ~

'Twas twilight,
all creatures
still ... at rest.

Slight breezes
gently warm
stirred 'round me.

Behind closed
eyes, wispy
visions formed ~

A voice from
far away ...
a low, soft

luring urge,
"Come, m'love,
here awaits

such dreams you
never knew
to exist."

Behind the Smile!

*Something in
my heart stirred;
primal urge*

*from ancient
passions soared ...
and I cried.*

(Freud Style)

You might...

...believe that you're not here with me
in everything I do,
but when I greet each morning sun
you're here to share it, too.

...think all I say and do is trite –
it's nothing but old news,
but I can promise You my sweet,
your touch cures all my blues.

...accept that there's no need to hope,
our future's looking dim ...
for every step we take we lose,
to You it's just a whim.

...no longer feel my touch so warm,
my breath upon your skin;
tho, I send all my love to You,
it flows no more within.

...believe it deeply saddens me
recalling how we've cared,
my thrill no longer takes You to
sweet moments that we've shared.

...conclude that after all the times
I speak to no reply,
I'd lose my love and move along,
forgetting how to try.

...take issue with the things I say,
and wish I would desist,
and if it were not for my love
for you ~ I could resist.

...not realize without You there
my world would fall apart;
and tho I'm hearing all your hints,
not so my in-love heart.

~_____~**~_____~

(Ballad)

IMAGERY

~ A Peaceful Hush ~

Through sheer lace curtains,
sunlight
greets mine eyes ...
to early dove song's
cooing calls
to rise.

— • —

A stretch, or two,
the shutters
then thrown wide ...
life's splend'rous wonders,
on display
outside.

— • —

Lies morning dew's
brocade,
spread 'cross the lawn ...
caught in each drop
glint sunbeams'
spark'ling dawn.

— • —

Imagery

Rise steamy mists
in ghostly
arabesques ...
stand floral colours,
tall and
statuesque.

— • —

Wends warmly through,
a gentle
breeze's brush ...
whilst all around
takes on
a peaceful hush.

(Mollietta)

NORTHERN LIGHTS ...

By wisps, ethereally solar wind
infuses in the skies a magic show;
with brilliance of atmospheric blend,
flow sheets of waving wonder to and fro.
Aurora Borealis in the north ...
oft' times displayed in beauty to the eye ...
soft shades of varied colors springing forth,
at sixty miles above the earth soar high;
the "Northern Lights" they have been aptly named;
down south, Aurora Austrialis known.
Pale green 'n blue, with shades of red they're flamed;
sometimes, with pink and violet are shown,
but most of all, in eerie yellow-green
of rippling curtained, shooting rays they're seen.

(English Sonnet)

These passion-filled dreams ~

Supine, they dream there, with nary a care,
upon the palms of their hands sparkles dance.
Their calm peaceful air, both fully aware ...
reposed, they embrace in soft, silent trance.

All throughout the night, wild fanciful flight ...
deft, sating fingers like hot, searing rain.
Alluring delight, so tender their plight;
seldom, thru dreamers sweeps such sweet refrain.

Then, come by 'n by, from sheer joy they cry;
tears shed deeply sad, yet from love they flow.
From each star-filled eye, sings life's lullaby,
to strike ebon night afire by their glow.

Darkness fear thee ne'er, 'cause out there somewhere,
love's pure, ribboned-ethers wispily bind;
for each of us e'er, there's one who will share,
these passion-filled dreams ~ each heart, soul, and mind.

(Fives 'n Tens)

Waking-up!

Aroused, I wake with smiles inside,
that ebb and flow like mystic tide;

each stretch and moan takes me away
beneath night's cover's disarray.

It is superb to lay supine...
to feel the blush of rush so fine,

as each and every place in me,
becomes sensatious jubilee;

so relaxed ... I can't help stalling,
tho, I hear day's urgent calling.

Waking-up can be ~ such pure bliss...
a wisp of heaven not to miss.

(Rhyming Couplets)

SADNESS

Beside the pond ~

~_____~**~_____~

Alone,
I sat beside the pond
this morning.

Early sun ...
vibrant in its warm flush
of golden welcome
came cascading down
from the treetops,
embracing grass and the awe in me,
gifting colors vividly alive,
lifting flowers' faces
with their honey-pollen smiles.

I was amazed
at how the breeze knew
I missed you
or was even thinking of you,
but I'd swear
it touched mine with your cheek,
slid a wisp of your locks
across my shoulder,
and became the sweetness
of your breath.

Sadness

*Olive oil and rose bouquet ...
it hung for awhile
in the morning air,
a fragrant marker
along a trail of yesterdays,
leading to You ...
places of dreams and hope,
of love and laughter
and impossible possibilities.*

*I almost started to believe
I'd turn my head ~
and you'd be there.*

*Each year
has come and gone ...
You, like fertile mana
ever glowing, growing
in my heart.*

*It's said all things end,
and walking back to the house,
I sensed the coming chill
when Autumn's leaves
fall like tears ~
washing around
my feet.*

(Free Verse)

Blessed from above ~

~**~

'Twas on that Spring night, two heart's soared in-flight
on gold wings sprouted then 'n there.
Such bliss they both knew, and rarely by few,
two souls who were reborn, I swear.

Her angel face glowed, sweet love was bestowed,
two hearts wed as one evermore.
Her heart was as pure, as his heart was sure
what God breathed life into him for.

Their gold wings entwined, while stars came aligned,
a course charted two lives would take.
Desires blended one, as warm as the sun,
each swearing they'll never forsake.

There was nothing spared, their ecstasy shared
a spark to ignite once cold blood.
Ne'er before had came such wild, fiery flame
to bloom full, their yellow rosebud.

Each heart, soul, and mind forever entwined,
frames mated in climax arched rush.
Warm, pearl rivers flowed ~ lovemaking bestowed
with passion that made the gods blush.

When wind-chimes ring bright some soft Summer night,
I'll soar high with You once again;
to Bolero, dance, in your green-eyed trance,
and taste your lips' endless champagne.

The mockingbird's trill, dove's soft cooing thrill,
in ways only lovers can hear.
This much is assured, no lovelier's heard
by woman or man's mortal ear ...

yet, time moves along, oft waning life's song
that sang in sweet voices of love.
Sure, we'll cry sad tears, but smile for our years ...
when we were once blessed from above ~

———————~**~———————————————

(Fives 'n Eights)

In Eternity ~ ~ ~ ~ ~ ~ ~ ~ ~ ~ ~ ~*

When there above yon tall pecans
the pale moon rises high,
cattails bend down softly to a breeze
and rushes wave a sad goodbye ...

there's an aching in my heart
that nothing can quite quell;
I wish you'd changed your mind,
and stayed a longer spell.

The whippoorwill, she beckons,
a song so sad and blue,
from every falling leaf your voice
is calling for me, too.

The turning of my heart,
each beat a lonely tune;
I know I'll never smile again
if You don't come back soon.

With lowered head I wander ...
down paths we strolled before,
and every stone your feet upturned,
remembered all the more.

Amongst the rows of evergreen
we swore our lover's vows;
then, carved our names into the bark
... made love beneath their boughs.

I hope you're happier than me,
that your new love treats you sweet;
and, every chance he has he takes
to make your happiness complete.

In Autumn's leaves I'll see your eyes,
golden waves of grain your hair,
in each and every cloud on high ...
images of your shape are there.

In every face on every street,
I'll look to see if it is You,
and with each breath that I take in,
there'll be enough for two.

No doubting now, nor can there be;
for, nevermore I'll be alone.
All through my veins your essence flows,
deep in my core and every bone.

Such blissful comfort sings to me
of Paradise in harmony,
that an angel's love sent from above
lives on forever ~ in eternity.

~ ~

(Unmetered Quatrains)

"LONELY BOY"

There once was
a boy quite good,
who had no love
but knew he should.
No love had the "Lonely Boy"

She found him,
kissed so softly ...
brought him joy,
opened the heart
of the "Lonely Boy"

She taught him faithfully;
then, set him free;
no love was lost for her ...
just another spree.
So, he died a "Lonely Boy"

His epitaph was written
in the stars above that shine:
She said, "I would have loved him
... IF ...
I'd only had the time!"

(Unmetered Quatrains w/Envois)

Lost Fate ...

'Twas once our hearts upon love's parchment danced,
in jubilee and joy our voices rang;
with tenderness and love, how we romanced,
and every song that could be sung ~ we sang.

On flagrant wings your poems all soared away
to others' hearts ... whomever they may be,
and onward rushes life in disarray,
with promise drowning in some heartless sea.

O' memories, embrace me one last time,
in comfort for lost years we shan't reclaim;
but, shed no tears to recompensing rhyme,
nor lack of knowing who or what to blame.

'Tis destiny unlocks life's waiting gate;
in truth, tho ... without You, I have no fate.

(English Sonnet)

Love's Ambling Seasons ~

When frozen limbs of Winter crack,
these arms ache empty, too ~
I close sad eyes...then, all drifts back
to days when dreams were true.

A time when summer held two hearts
within it's youthful sway...
each mem'ry dances, then departs;
too quickly drifts away.

Through Autumn's glory, life we strolled,
soft wind-chimes knew our song...
sweet poems writ 'pon leaves of gold;
'twas naught e'er could go wrong.

Sweet spring waltzed in on verdant wing,
brought laughter in the rain...
then summer's bliss began to sing
to fall's poignant refrain.

Each falling leaf a melody
that played upon two hearts...
each drop of rain brought destiny,
as love slowly departs.

Sadness

We sensed the paling of desire,
a waning of each thrill...
and barely kindled sparks of fire
to weather winter's chill.

Tho' our love's seasons ambled by,
the mem'ry's seldom stilled;
nor, moments two hearts soaring high...
were e'er, alas – fulfilled.

(Ballad)
Cowrite w/L.Charlyne Zurick © 22 Jan 2012
                                      Permission granted.

Lovers' Lament

Hallowed and grand he felt her hand,
as it caressed his fevered brow.
With rev'rent bow, he knew (somehow)
he was a destined man.
An angel's touch, he knew that such
meant she and heaven had come near.
The air, it spun, warmed by the sun;
'twas then he knew God's plan.

In soft rejoice, deep with a voice
of love, He'd bade the robin sing;
then, with a gush of vibrant rush
his world was set aglow!
Oh, Lady Faire, with golden hair,
eyes em'rald as the verdant lea;
hearts wedded true, pledged then by two
their love would always grow.

Fair seasons came, but ne'er the same ...
deep, promised vows two lovers spake.
Too many gales and storm worn sails
had rent their vessel's worth.
Sensitive ways, un-mended days,
they both had tried their very best.
Alas, they knew that they were through;
love died before its birth.

(Char's 3 + 1)

Our Love's Seasons ~

When frozen limbs of Winter crack,
these arms ache empty, too –
I close sad eyes ... then, all drifts back
to days when dreams were true.

A time when Springtime held two hearts
within it's youthful sway ...
each mem'ry dances, then departs;
too quickly drifts away.

Through Autumn's glory, life we strolled,
soft wind-chimes knew our song ...
sweet poems writ 'pon leaves of gold;
'twas naught e'er could go wrong.

Sweet Spring waltzed in on verdant wing,
brought laughter in the rain ...
then Summer's bliss began to sing
to Fall's poignant refrain.

Each falling leaf a melody
that played upon two hearts ...
each drop of rain brought destiny,
as love slowly departs.

Behind the Smile!

We sensed the paling of desire,
a waning of each thrill ...
and barely kindled sparks of fire
to weather Winter's chill.

Tho' our love's seasons ambled by,
memory's seldom stilled;
nor, moments two hearts soaring high ...
were e'er, alas – fulfilled.

(Ballad)

Sad Ink ~

B'neath yon tallow ... wiling way the day,
where past has come a'wand'ring through my mind,
of all t'was learned and done along the way ...
how so much more is left out there to find.
For every bit of wisdom I have learned,
recalling each good deed I've ever done,
so many times the midnight oil has burned
to scribe my poems – dusk to rising sun.
An olde bard now, 'tis much that I regret;
there's been more, too, of which I feel quite glad.
Still, looking back and on what's coming, yet ...
here's hoping I'll be happier than sad.

   Those poets whose ink's from a broken heart,
   are destined to write sadness ~ from the start!

(English Sonnet)

Behind the Smile!

Softly ~ in my dreams...

Days turn to pain I cannot show,
nights into ever-endless streams.
Reaching to find I'm lonely; though,
I hold you Softly ~ in my dreams.

My days now empty without you,
to nights no peace will come, it seems;
for your touch ache the long night through,
I'll hold you Softly ~ in my dreams.

Where's gone your shelter for my storm,
what of love spent...in lifetime schemes,
when all turns cold, who'll keep me warm?
I'll hold you Softly ~ in my dreams.

Who'll grasp the beauty of my mind,
then thrill my body to extremes,
or take my hand when I am blind?
I'll hold you Softly ~ in my dreams.

When scared, no one to hold me tight.
Oh, I shall know what life redeems ...
when all else dims, you'll be my light.
I'll hold you Softly ~ in my dreams.

(Kyrielle)

~ THE DANCE ~

... to karma ...

Within this empty hall I live
This place inside my skin,
Home to my darkest direst faults
Unchaste shadows to unanswered sin.

~ .*. ~

Pondering upon these vile notions
That keep returning ever in me,
Forever asking how I'm so smart
While my own soul's not yet free.

~ .*. ~

Music composed by my sorted life
Continues to hauntingly play,
Toe begins tapping that rhythm
As my body begins to sway.

~ .*. ~

Legs unwilling all under me now
I'm gliding 'round this empty room,
Dancing forever to an un-tuned chorus
To chords of this dark, askew doom.

~ .*. ~

When was the time I went wrong
Was there one certain start?
Sliding along now shuffling toes
In silent time to an off-beat heart.

~ .*. ~

Behind the Smile!

~ .*. ~

Each note a deed I've done
That I can never be proud,
Fingers now snapping quickly
Ragged music playing too loud.

~ .*. ~

Cymbals clash in tinny refrain
Metallic taste on my tongue,
Strums of a guitar far away
Words to songs long ago sung.

~ .*. ~

Cannot stop stepping though I must
My feet have been worn so thin,
Oh, no! Not another bad song
I can't keep doing this endless dance....

~ .*. ~

....AGAIN 'N AGAIN....

———————=•~ .*. ~•=———————

-=~ .*. ~=-

•

.

(Unmetered Quatrains)

"For every deed committed, every action dark or bright,
there is an energy created ... remaining in us – exuding from us ...
and it is that which remains, returning again and again,
until we receive equal or make suitable amends!"

Unacknowledged Phantom Lover
Why, of course....!

The veil just lifted,
revealing so pure and crystal-clear,
that vision you've all-along
been trying to show me,
Dear.

My eyes are opened now,
at long-last I can see,
that sad, laughable clown,
that's been lingering there....

Hah-ha-hah!
But, wait!
... Oh, no! ...

How could I
have gotten it so wrong....
not to have seen it
all before?

It is really no clown, at-all,
just a harmless,
and lonely old bard,
left behind,

Behind the Smile!

sitting, bent over his worn desk,
throughout dark and day.

Tarnished pen,
poised in gentle care,
held lovingly between toil-bent fingers,
deeply creased, his rugged hand,
clean, crisp parchment....

"Only the best will do
for Her," he thought.

Awaiting his pleasure,
hopeful dreams to be shared,
for his heart to be joined to hers
in gleeful, warm embrace,
together again ... once more
as they'd soared gracefully,
as they had
so many times before.

Love poems to be....
written in golden ink – his tepid blood
pumped from deep within his core,
his tender heart and soul,
forevermore steeped
in loyal splendor.

He sits ... he labors,
pouring forth life's soul,
the stars in his eyes turned wonderment,
of vivid dreams to be.

Sweet dedications to his beloved darling....
so many the time she'd refrained,
"I'll be your unforgettable forevermore,
your beautiful brightest star...!"
She, now, but his eternal,
unacknowledged phantom lover.

(Free Verse)

Whisper Of Shadows ~

The hunger in
her eyes begin
to dwell on all
we'd soon forestall ...
that made cheeks blush
with each swift rush,
of blood's careen
all in-between,
to make sublime
mem'ry of time;
no heresy,
to be set free
in soul's barren
lack of sharin'.
No passion's flame ...
night's silence came:
"Oh, nocturnal
garland vernal,
sweet love we knew
shared by so few,
where did it go?
I have to know;
it's faded to ...
yesterday's echo!"

(Cywydd Devair Fyrion, w/Envoi)

Written with air.............*

There may come a time
when thoughts dissipate,
like frost that lingered
as lace on green blades;
and, like early dew,
you are no longer here,
inside my mind, my soul ...
when my heart has thawed,
after sun's warmth has
bowed in encore.

Where have our moments gone,
those that called us out to dance,
to sweetly embrace it all,
to revel in the afterglow of laughter,
to shine with the tears of forgiveness;
and, what of all the gold we shared,
our hours spent
in ethereal lovemaking?

I knew you — oh, so well ...
the child of you,
the woman in you, too,
and all that life called us to be,
together ~
in the spark of eternal
forevermore.

Behind the Smile!

Our days and nights,
spent wrapped in splendor,
thrust together,
entwined like vines
with insatiable fingers ...
swimming your pools
of vibrant depths,
those portals into
your soul.

It is as though ...
a mystical wand passed over us,
and like the sigh
of a baby's first breath,
here, in soft feathered touch.

Hah!
Gone now,
forevermore ...
as if we, You and I,
were merely ~
Written with air.............*

(Free Verse)

HUMOR

A Smile!

The ol' tomcat, he sauntered-up one night;
then, made himself at home ... like he belongs.
He's grouchy and demanding, with a spite;
then, sings each eve his wily tomcat songs.

His mood is far less than congenial,
and every time I try to pet his fur,
he gives a growl that's aboriginal;
no doubt he is disgruntled, that's for sure.

He chases all the animals away,
to claim the choicest lounging spots as his.
There's no denying he demands his way,
and tells the others everything that is.

I'd had enough of cold, cantank'rous wile ...
when his soft, purring nudge gifts me ~ a smile!

(English Sonnet)

As I grew olde ...

I soon began to mould, as I grew olde ...
'twas not quite in the way that you might think.
Some say my colours, they've turned less than bold,
and how my thoughts no longer seem to synch.

I tell you true – there's not much left to find;
what looks I had the clock's now washed away,
left naught but bawdy thoughts to rule the mind,
and all I want to do is flirt and play.

"Now, (what)," I ask, "is there left to enjoy,
and what faire damsel being chased by me,
is gonna want for me to be her toy;
an olde bard, trying yet to soar hearts free?"

The mould, you see, is not from wrinkled years,
but by salt shed from all your laughter's tears.

(English Sonnet)

‡┈┈\#~‼CONNIPTION‼~#/┈┈‡
~* frustrated ♩ humor •~

*

Seems lately I been bothered
By every this and that,
Fault found in everything
Just spoilin' for a spat.

~ # ~

Damn those barkin' dogs
Neighbor mowin' too early when,
Those crazy crows keep cawing
Over and over – again and again.

~ @ ~

I've about had it with the phone
It rings from eight till five,
The bills keep coming-in
It's small wonder I'm alive.

~ % ~

Why is that cabinet door
Again left wide ajar,
Get that damned cat off
My shiny fresh-washed car.

~ ¿ ~

Who has left the light on
Why do you never learn,
How to close the door
Slowly I'm beginning to burn.

~ i ~

Where are the car-keys
Not where they're supposed to be,
I'll never know why dysfunction
Has come to live with me.

~ ¥ ~

The lid is again left off
Can't get my words to rhyme,
I've come to the conclusion
That's it's just about that time.

~ ø ~

For me to blow a gasket
By virtue of this description,
Run screaming round the house
Into the yard on down the road
...in a wildly-laughing, hysterical...

‡——/#~CONNIPTION!~#/——‡

" • ~*#*~ • "

*

(Unmetered Quatrains)

"When little things build up and it all begins closing-in,
sometimes a fit is all that will dispel it adequately.
Everyone run for the hills; because, "Here One Comes!" ☺

"FIRST KISS"
(true story)

Hmm? Try as I might,
she was so very shy
I may as well have
been saying goodbye.

For, she was having
none of this scamp,
she was the school's
prim proper vamp.

Who kept her eyes
always lowered down,
when I came a-flirtin'
she'd just turn around.

I cajoled and I winked
acted proper 'n smiled,
tried to tote her books
ignored, like a bad child.

Of course, she was right
at the time, I admit,
only for fighten 'n cussin'
back then was I fit.

But, I persevered grandly
as boys love-struck often do,
and in diligent, due time
my sweetheart came through.

'Twas the junior-prom night
I came a-callin' all spiffed,
she was a fairy-tale princess
my true heart's little gift.

I met mom and dad
(with their suspicions galore),
and they were quite right
soon's we got out the door.

In the awkward glitch
of a fifteen year old,
my move on her lips
seemed just a bit bold.

So, she stuck her hand
right square in my face,
hurt my tender feelings
but, my plan, it did not displace.

For, to an eager young mind
the night was yet new,
it all was worked out
just what we would do.

Behind the Smile!

After the dance ... all alone
in my dad's loaned me car,
I was convinced my charms
would take me quite far.

Then, the band struck-up
on the floor we rubbed thighs,
as we dipped 'n we whirled
I could see in her eyes.

That my plan was working
tonight was the one sure,
the back seat would be
the un-flowering of her.

Then, we sat down to eat
it all was going so fine,
the banquet featured steak;
she was lookin' like mine.

And, I had her ... I knew it
she sat down at my right,
and smiled so sweetly.
Yesh! This was the big night!

I grabbed my knife 'n fork.
commenced with carving mishap,
that tough old steak slipped-off
the plate ... right onto her lap.

She looked down in silence;
then, out with a shrill scream;
then, I knew for sure
'twas the end of my dream.

White, full-formal gown
steak sauce did now adorn,
as she ran bawlin' right by
in her eyes there was scorn.

And, 'twas not the mistake
I had made got her cryin',
but the incessant way we all
laughed 'til we were dyin'.

Try sincerely as I might
all-apologetic and remiss,
me and Dad's backseat
never got ... that first kiss.

    (Unmetered Quatrains)

"GOBBLE! GOBBLE!"
(a Thanksgiving story)

Didn't you really know just how
I was always happy to see only you,
How you'd make me wobble so fast
Peeping with an excited ruffle or two.

How I ever-so faithfully followed
Your long strides and then,
You would so fondly turn and pet me
Bringing water and feed to my pen.

Those long past years
I had mostly steadily grown,
To love and trust you as if
I had become like one of your own.

You'd kept me warm and comfy
Ever since I was just a small chick,
For you I would strut so proudly
Always knowing I was your favorite pick.

Suddenly, things seemed so different
That day you acted so oddly askew,
I sure hoped I hadn't fallen into disfavor
Or become a disappointment to you.

"I know!"...I said
"I'll puff-up and strut for you awhile!"
When you see how hard I'm trying
It's sure to bring back your lost smile.

It seemed quite strange this caring effort
Was making me think, "What the heck!"
When you rushed in to hug me but missed
And grabbed me twisting my neck.

"Gobble! Gobble!" as I faded
Is all you could hear me say,
But my broken heart was crying
"How can you treat me this way?"

(to "Peepers")

1983-88

(Unmetered Quatrains)

"This is about a pet turkey named "Peepers,
because she peeped all the time – like turkeys do.
I didn't really wring her neck, as the poem infers.
I only ended it this way for interest's sake, so don't be sad.
She just grew old and died. She was sweet and a fun friend!
Missing her now! :'(

Gud eatin'!

I have just now spied a chap named Chip,
who saw me comin' and took a dip
down back into his hole...
met-up with Mister Mole,
who said, "I guess you just gave the slip

to that hungry ol' mean-lookin' guy,
who was sizin' ya up with his eye."
Good it is that you did,
if not – heaven forbid...
you'd end up cooked in his Chipmunk pie!

(English Limerick Doublet)

Jus' Kuntry Fun!

I slid-up in the old pickup,
dust stirrin' wild, 'n beeped tha horn!
you ran so fast, with skirt askance;
jus' kuntry fun 'n wild romance!

Ya hugged my neck real tight 'n good,
and planted one right on my cheek!
You made me smile and my heart dance;
jus' kuntry fun 'n wild romance!

You call it whatever ya like;
it don't make me no nevermind.
All I knows is...I'm in her trance;
jus' kuntry fun 'n wild romance!

I shift to low and hit the gas,
off to the barn dance for some fun.
Okay, quit playin' with my pants;
jus' kuntry fun 'n wild romance!

We might not make it to the barn,
the pond 'n grass-bank's lookin' swell.
I think it's time we took a chance;
jus' kuntry fun 'n wild romance!

Behind the Smile!

Off-a-tha road we veered real quick
toward that spot I'll lay you down.
Tree hit! Your thighs I took a glance;
jus' kuntry fun 'n wild romance!

The truck, she's gone, it's her last day...
we never did arrive that night.
'Twere bound to happen, 'cause perchance;
jus' kuntry fun 'n wild romance!

The months slipped by, we swore our vows.
Ol' stork's arrived, and two are three.
Our love life's now about finance,
jus' kuntry fun 'n wild romance!

(Two-Step)

I had in mind a love poem when I took pen to hand, but look what it turned into ... go figure! LOL!

Who's to know what direction, or to what kind of fancy a poet's mind will turn, eh?

"Try it, you might like it, too!"

LAZY, CRAZY MAYZIE

I've heard that Mayzie is quite lazy;
about as languid as a daisy.

For my part I conclude ...
not meaning to be rude:

I'm thinking Mayzie's mostly crazy!

(English Limerick)

....-=LOST..COOKIES=-....
~ Mm! ~

...-= ;) =-...

She heated that old oven
butter'd that old pan,
With tender love and care
rolled them in her hand.

...-=-...

Slid them in the oven
tapped toes to anticipation,
Waiting for them to rise
gifts fill her imagination.

...-=-...

He'll simply love these
my big strong loving boy,
When he sees how hard I've tried
his heart will skip with joy.

...-=-...

She chose the strongest box
that had the tightest lid,
Cushioned them with care
covered with kindness she did.

...-=-...

...-=-...

Wrapped it up with colors
blue and red and green,
Twas the most beautiful box
she had ever seen.

...-=-...

Gave it to the postman
stamped Handle It With Care,
Send these to my loved-one
my heart with him I share.

...-=-...

She waited and she wondered
when time had finally passed,
That they should have arrived
and he'd be calling her at last.

...-=-...

Her phone, it did not ring
no thanks for cookies yummy,
He waited daily at the mailbox – alas
seems they were delivered by mistake

to

the mailman's tummy!

.....~•=•~.....
*

(Unmetered Quatrains w/Envoi)
....just a fun little bit of holiday humor....

`;.•:*~ 'Midsummer Dreamin'~*:•.;`

`;.•:*~*:•.;`

Here bummin' barefoot on the beach,
I've just now found a vantage spot;
so many lovelies in my reach,
each one of them is lookin' hot.

"";*;""

Some sassy – others quite demure,
here bummin' barefoot on the beach;
spry 'n young – MMmmm...sweetly mature,
but ne'er a one who's not a peach.

"";*;""

She purred, "Hi, Boy!" (oops! lost my speech),
so she kept swaying right on by.
Here bummin' barefoot on the beach,
how many more will catch my eye?

"";*;""

Each one is gorgeous in their form;
I'm sure there's much they all could teach.
Inside, my raging hormones storm,
here bummin' barefoot on the beach.

"";*;""

(French Quatern)

Naughty 'n Nice!

*I stayed up all night,
wrapped each present tight,*

*tied ribbons of silk;
poured your glass of milk.*

*Now, I know I should
been a bit more good,*

*but I'm just a man
doin' the best he can.*

*Please, don't fault me hard;
this fun-natured bard*

*and fond ladies' play...
make our days more gay.*

*Surely, there's no harm,
free-sharing our charm;*

*we share cuddles, too,
I'll promise it's true.*

Behind the Smile!

So, Dear Santa, see...
while she trims the tree,

top star's lifted high;
then, should (by-and-by)

a shy peek up there,
per mere chance I swear,

holding her ladder,
what can it matter,

a quick glimpse of thigh?
One might quand'ry why

would she climb up there,
knowin' sure I'd stare?

Naughty boy, it's true,
but if it were you,

and if you were me
with her by that tree,

I'm thinking you would,
think that naughty's good.

Sweet cookies 'n milk,
presents tied with silk,

come nigh Christmas night
before your great flight,

My name's on her list,
it's "Naughty Boy Kissed."

Then, read what she wrote
in her little note,

"Oh, Sweet Santa Dear,
This time every year,

Merry Christmas, cause You
are my naughty boy, too!"

Wink*

(Rhyming Couplets)

The Witch's Blush

When I was but a young warlock,
with witches played and did cavort.
Partaking they my wizard's stock...
crones young 'n old made me their sport.

Each shouting, "Terminus a quem!"
cast o'er me spells, wild spewing chants,
took me behind 'pon rides with them;
"Zing!" when aroused, off went my pants.

This warlock learned a thing (or two)
of just how to enchant a witch.
When witches get zonked on their brew,
watch close, you'll see long noses twitch.

Right after that they curse and swear,
then cackle loud with eerie glee.
Reach 'neath and steal their underwear!
Shout these words as you quickly flee,

"I saw your all and it was grand!"
and she will know that something's wrong;
mounting her broom she'll understand....
the wind will tell her, "There's no thong!"

(Unmetered Quatrains)

Wet Dream!
lil' bit naughty! ;)

I dreamt last night you came to me
and kissed me on the lips.
You lay atop me soft and warm,
I felt my heart turn flips.

There was no doubt of your intent,
as warmth rose up my thighs ...
and as it did your hand did too,
quite much to my surprise.

I kept on laying silently,
as sleepers mostly will ...
and when I felt my passions rise,
I tried to lay real still.

It was so hard, but I still tried,
and growing harder yet.
I swear I felt your thighs each side,
between 'twas warm and wet

It was too much to not awake,
and did to my sad dread;
never again too much water ...
before I go to bed!

(Quatrains in 8/6 Count)

JAPANESE FORMS

blossom

delicate petals
meandering gentle hosts
cherished blossom time

(Haiku)

Dating Details!
(he asked her)

How do you like sex?
I like it infrequently!
That's one word or two?

(Senryu)

f a t e

tiny flame-flickers
piercing farthest deepest dark
life's wings seduced to unfurl
flitting circling
drawn ever nearer each beat
gossamer spanning veins burnt
falling in spirals
eternal alluring sighs
thus love's dreams each borning die

(Sedoka)

Japanese forms

(first taste)

Biscuit aroma;
oh-MY! Blackberry preserves.
Fresh, home-churned butter.
Loo's calling first, "Hurry up!"
"Good day," gifts morning's promise.

(Tanka)

(God's canvas)

'Neath diamond glints,

every rolling contour blessed,

festooned mysteries . . .

strokes caresse dy loving hands

upon Earth's warm, verdant lands.

(Tanka)

(winter pages)

hard cool breezes breathe
soaring leaves flutter to rest
hue strewn forest floor

textures richly mute
bare limbs buttress pale gray skies
autumn now lives here

snowflakes maundering
bright the mantle cold and clean
winter reigns anon

(Haiku Suite)

KATANA

the samurai soul

forged folded tempered by fire

victorious dreams

(Senryu)

Life-thirst...

Billowed clouds on high,
glorious, fluffy heights form;
pure white – soon growing darker,
by liquid life filled,
they prepare to serve their worth ... oblivious to all death.

Above, all observed
by sun's heart's bright shining warmth ...
awaiting its turn to give.
Below, praying hope
embraced; all cold dissipates ...
bestowed – every need its due.

(Sedoka Doublet)

Behind the Smile!

(lofty mantle)

earthlands cloaked with warmth
clouds aloft in gentle breeze
sun-brushed golden rays

(Haiku)

Japanese forms

~ meeting and departing ~

Life introduced us ...
felt, your faint, inviting smile.

~=*=~

Words exchanged ~ minds spoke.

~=*=~

The truth, answered now in full
our foray ... our completion.

(Tanka)

"There are relationships both know are not to be ~
yet, for one (or both) of them it can be arduous to let go.
May you forevermore dance upon soft wind."

Behind the Smile!

(the cure)

its the gift to give
a man who has everything
penicillin shot

(Senryu)

Japanese forms

(snowflakes falling)

soft silent snowflakes
falling like lace crystal wings
drift into my heart

(Senryu)

Behind the Smile!

(seasons)

staunchly without fail
each season guarding nature
cedes to naught but time

(Haiku)

Death's Lure...

No freedom exists!
Though, escaping my cocoon,
I must seek you once again;
I am drawn to you
like a moth to its candle,
circling ever nearer...
lured into your flame.
Trusting wings now seared, I fall.
What is this force that endures?

(Choka)

Behind the Smile!

You know something, gal?
~ steaming love ~

~=*=~

You know something, gal,
this, I've been wanting to say,
"There is no true love like ours."

~=•=~

On the other hand,
when thinking of our egos,
"It shows why we've shared little."

~=*=~

(Sedoka)
~ so frustrating when we have it, but can't gift it ~

PROMISE

~ A Brand New Start ~

Oh, come thee joyful to these waiting arms,
embrace my soul within your glory's grace.
Fill me, my love, with all your sweetest charms.
Spread wide this gentle smile across my face.
I'd spent a life in hopeful search to find
what heaven's brought together from above;
the ones who truly fit with warmth in-kind,
and never have you gone back on your love.
Life 'pon us did this miracle decree ...
that you and I forever come to know,
from far across love's deep, alluring sea,
where life has led and means for us to go.
Ne'er beat like this before ... my old, worn heart,
until fate gifted us - a brand-new start.

(English Sonnet)

....at the altar of Your love ~

When I spoke, no one could hear
when I reached, no one to feel,
when I cried, there flowed no tear
and when I loved, it felt unreal.

When I moved, there was no motion
when I looked, no one was there,
when I trusted, none to lean on
and when I pled, no one to care.

The other night, as I was thinking
only pain had come my way,
no matter where this mind took me
there was but sorrow and dismay.

So, I climbed deep inside those walls
where I'd dwelt so many times before,
there in that dark 'n shadowed world
where light called out to me no more.

Where only coldness sought my soul
to come into that nether realm,
hard-cursed promises, dire unease
gripped deep sadness to overwhelm.

Yet, in those days live my bygones
where hopes of love and splendor came,
but to be crushed again each time
smothered, I hung my head in shame.

Behind the Smile!

Afraid to take another chance
even when with love they came along,
each and every time in earnest tried
something forever went so wrong.

As this crumpled image I'd become
stood entombed within that wall,
all life then over in my heart
time to partake life's ultimate fall.

In that dire, decisive moment when
the choice to end lay finally made,
appeared such warmth only dreamt of
in desperate times when I had prayed.

Ensued mighty fights and struggles
inside this empty, hollow man,
until You became the eternal spark
of new life for Us then began.

Now, when I speak, I am heard
when I reach, then deeply felt,
and when I cry it is real tears; for
....at the altar of Your love~ I've knelt.

~~~~~~~~~~~~~~~~~~~~~~~\~**\~~~~~~~~~~~~~~~~~~~~~~

(Unmetered Quatrains)

For loving me.... Thank You!

~=~BE AT PEACE~=~

-=~**~=-

For...there is a heart
Out here
Somewhere
That wants to share
Your care
Your fear
Your tear
Your cheer
Anytime, anywhere
So come on over here
Just cuddle with me, Dear
In this chair
'Cause I swear
That I'll be there
To brush your hair
Answer your prayer
Calm your nightmare
With love to spare
And, more to share

~:~

I solemnly swear!

-=~**~=-

~ | ~

*

(Skeltonic Verse)

~~~~~ BREEZE ~~~~~

~~~~~§~~~~~

As morning's golden glow surrenders ~ skies azure,
heat a'rise, light wind lifting softly, wafting pure.

~~ • ~~

Flowers' faces, each turning t'ward the beauty there,
branches dancing gently, upon the rising air.

~~ • ~~

Sleeping spirits awaken, warming their cold breast,
softly, doves are cooing, birds singing in their nests.

~~ • ~~

Squirrels' eager chatter calls mates, high up in trees,
tender touch to my face, in my heart...oh, sweet breeze!

~~ • ~~

Carry to me gently, my dreams, desires and more,
that you'll e'er be my ocean; me, your willing shore.

~~ • ~~

Flow around and through me, soaring wings free my heart,
soothe my soul...glory's passions, nevermore we'll part.

~~ • ~~

Together, we'll traverse God's apex ~ beauty grand,
Wend through every niche and nook 'cross His great land.

~~ • ~~

Oh, carry me to bed each eve, before you sleep.
Sweep o'er me one last time, our paradise to keep.

~~ • ~~

Around this yearning frame wrap wispy arms, my pleas...
that, on each morrow we soar as one ~ love's sweet breeze.

~~~~~§~~~~~

(Rhyming Couplets)

~=~Fate's Door~=~

Across yon ebon stretch of sky I see
amazement far beyond all ever dreamed;
not viewed by eyes, but deep within my soul,
an open portal beckons, "Enter, you'll find Me!"

Why am I haunted by this mystery;
why is the world no longer as it seemed,
why am I half, when once I'd felt quite whole;
life's plan I know we cannot know, but why taunt me?

I'll bide my time until my spirit's free,
when on that day – I'll know what Chance has deemed
recorded endlessly upon life's scroll ...
unlocked, fate's door now, by The Master's golden key.

(Tenz on 12)

Gift us wings ~

Into yon azure sky,
ye ever gaze up high
'pon bluebirds passing by;
then, wonder why it is they fly?

"'Tis beauty," I decry!
This much I can't deny;
fact is, to my mind's eye,
nay less to sky ... winged lullaby."

"Our sorrows purify,"
exclaimed a softened sigh!
"Pray, gift us flight," their cry,
"our souls soar high ... 'pon new wings spry!"

(Tripps O'er Quads)

Missive from Your Muse ~

Oh, how your Muse's heart, it gently turns,
as through your pen two spirits are set free ...
his flame of life from yours forever burns,
the muse he is to You ~ You are to He.

The star You gaze upon that brightly gleams,
no other does he shine for high above;
'tis right that he's the one who lights your dreams.
for ~ only "You" have taught him how to love.

And, as your Muse, he watches from on high,
aware that he is but a simple bard;
he knows well, too, the wand'rings of your eye,
that in your heavens, many there have starred.

Yet, I'm the star you've wrought ... we shine the same;
God's placed us there ~ to burn as one bright flame.

(English Sonnet)

"Our Living Sea of Destiny ~"

We each are living reservoirs
designed as such, made to be filled
with whatever life shall bring,
until our longings have been stilled.

So, open wide, receive it all
that sets our hearts and souls aglow,
and when full, look until we've found
the one in whom to overflow.

Fill them up with all you've drank
until they flow back into you ...
lifelong rivers ever merging bind
into one sea that once was two.

Once quiet waters stir and blend
with rising rolling to and fro.
No way to make them two again;
this is the only way they know.

At times their surface still and smooth,
others a sparkling sunlit rill;
then, tossed with dancing peaks a'churn,
to frothy waves that pound and thrill.

Breezes blow cool, soft sunlight warms,
each star a glint 'pon moonlit peaks.
With passion grows each pitch and roll;
while all abounds, a lifetime seeks.

Within us teems and never halts,
like ever-charging waves to shore;
our living sea of destiny ~
flows deep and wide ... forevermore.

(Quatrains in 8-Count)

Behind the Smile!

Remembrance

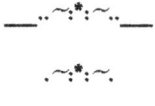

As life returns softly in time
to touch that living in my soul,
it matters not what comes in rhyme
only that life has left me whole.

the world now unfolds before me
As life returns softly in time,
remembrance of bygone pasts flee
warmly to realms recalled sublime.

Called on by nature in my prime
'twas life and love then danced as one,
As life returns softly in time
those days like flowers in the sun.

You pledged your heart and love so sweet
upon romantic wings we'd climb,
'midst heavenly stars our hearts meet
As life returns softly in time.

(French Quatern)

SEEKING

~ never give-up your dream ~

Maybe it's only amazement
That can capture the soul,
Or sell us on answers
To questions we hold.

—//—

Feeling ourselves
On the inside in time,
Finding ladders we've built
Too hard to climb.

—//—

Then don once again
The clearness of thought,
Surrendering in ease to
Warm comfort we've sought.

—//—

While worrying too much
Of timeless waste,
Not knowing all's not lost
That's been found in haste.

—//—

–//–
Left now to search again
For sought final goal,
Is amazement contained
In the heart of a true
Seeking soul.
————————//————————

(Unmetered Quatrains)
"Quitting is the one thing unnecessary to succeed."

Sometimes ~

Sometimes ~ when twilight falls, lying awake,
pure image of your face I'll contemplate;
then, loneliness ... my heart beats with such ache
no fantasy of You will compensate.

Sometimes ~ a sadness sweeps throughout my soul ...
forlorn, with wispy, dark clouds gath'ring low;
soft, blue skies form, a gentle breeze ~ I'm whole!
All life becomes a tender, warming glow.

Sometimes ~ I know and never shall forget,
while other times I wonder what fate holds,
but always, sings my heart a minuet ...
sweet rose bouquet our every word enfolds.

Sometimes ~ beside our pond I'll dream awhile,
content within the country of your smile ~

(English Sonnet)

~~ Sweet Valentine ~~

Your beauty is far too deep, ever to deceive,
with statuesque legs, sane minds can't believe.

Yes, the sun's too dim to outshine your glow,
and heaven's blessed your heart ~ like purest snow.

Angels shaped your face, roses brushed your lips.
It took God's hands to sculpt your luscious hips.

When You exhale, the bees all buzz with sighs.
Gentle loving hues bless your soul-deep eyes.

From deepest mysteries, came your silky hair.
Moonbeams set your skin aglow, so soft and fair.

Your supple breasts, ripe melons from the field,
so full and round, such joyfulness they yield.

Wisdom of ages grace your regal mind.
Your eloquence, a lifetime's perfect find.

From your touch, the meaning of compassion.
In your heart is found love's ideal fashion.

Now, all feels warm, when once so sad and cold.
Sweet Valentine, in You ~ all my dreams unfold.

(Rhyming Couplets)

THE BLUEBIRD

~ teach me ~

If I come a fledgling bluebird
will you teach me how
to sing;
when I've fallen from my nest
will you mend my
broken-wing?

If I land upon your shoulder
fly my way into
your heart,
will you let me know your love's
safe haven ~ nevermore
we'll part?

If I learn to love and trust you,
bring you twigs from
tender bough...
will you hold me gently to your breast,
my joyous songs will
you allow?

Behind the Smile!

Will your heart soar to see me fly
as I glide aloft upon our
drafts sublime,
my wings spread in proudest glory,
showing my love for you
each time?

———~*~———

When winter's snows have fallen,
will I find you there
to share,
for all my life to you
give all I have,
my beauty
my wings
my voice
*

... and yet ...
*

will you really
always
care?
*

———————————:~·~*~·~:———————————

(Free Style)
"Trust for and dedication to another living-being is commitment
never to take lightly or for granted ~ The heart and soul
are truly fragile things to take into one's care."

...THE • CHOICE...
~ souls...hearts know ~

........——.>~<.——...

Oh, MY Love....
When the winds of fortune,
Blow our hearts,
To and fro like leaves...
Upon
The breeze.

It is then,
We long for a soft,
A gentle place –
To land,

Because...
We know,
When the wind subsides...
We shall fall.

Yet, do we know...
Can we,
Where that will be,
When it will be?
We Cannot

Yet...
From this understanding,
We can perceive
What lies ahead
And choose wisely

...or...

Otherwise
By wiser
Choice.

I embrace your words,
I love your heart,
I enter your soul;
Then, here I am...

With you and without you,
Alone with me...
In body,

Never alone...
In love,
In our hearts and souls,
Intertwined are
We
...in every way...

We, the choice made...
and
Oh, yes!
What a heavenly choice
It so lovingly...

*

-= IS =-

*

.

(Free Verse)

"The heart, the soul, the love of two that are each others' glow
knows no boundary
only that it all dances between them sublimely-true!"

.~*The Flower In Your Hands*~.

...~**~...

I have looked upon you
now I see you well
and I've known you....woman & child

.~:~.

My heart soars at a mere thought;
the imagination of your hand on mine
gentle moistness of your lips

*

... or ...

*

just to rest within your gaze

.~:~.

I can often feel you inside me
and rest in comfort there

.~:~.

How can I forget the presence of life around me
when you are
to symbolize it all

.~:~.

How could I ignore the need of one so deserving
as yourself

.~:~.

.~:~.

What walled you from the world
opened your eyes to me

.~:~.

Taught me the need of giving
although I am not mine to give
whatever love I have
is yours to share

.~:~.

And I am ever grateful
for I have touched....ever so gently

*

.~*The Flower In Your Hands*~.

*

...~**~...

.~:~.

*

.

(Free Verse)

This Happy Song's for You!

Fill your heart with gladness,
sing this happy song:
"Shoo away all sadness,
rid yourself of all that's wrong.

Cry no more tears of sorrow,
let the sunshine in;
look forward to tomorrow,
and face it with a grin.

Allow love to embrace you,
open your arms wide;
there's someone who is true,
so let them come inside.

See the joy on flowers' faces,
hear soft laughter in the air;
let it into all your places,
there's so much love to share!"

Captured by the alluring bleat,
of love's soft, enchanting fife ...
stand and dance on happy feet,
to the primal tune of life.

When you feel love's sweet caress,
sigh, then, and smile all through;
be warmly willing to confess,
this happy song's for You!

(Unmetered Quatrains)

Tho' Many Unfulfilled....

Oh, starlight enthralling
glow's lavish befalling
'pon lovers' fantasy ...
girls rarely disagree.

In romance glorified,
e'er naïve, starry-eyed;
boys gazing heavenly
are praying serenely.

In heartfelt loneliness
they'll always reminisce,
of laughter departed
from being fainthearted.

So, listen patiently ...
then, attend faithfully,
or remain affected
when sadly rejected.

They're ever expecting,
but rarely connecting.

(Rhopalic Verse)

"TO BE YOUR MAN"
~ aspire ~

When I was but a fallow lad
Filled with lofty dreams...naïve ideals
The world turned a different speed – somehow

Then, the stars and trees caught my attention
The way your loving eyes haunt my soul
The splendor that is your skirt
Emphasizing the zenith of your hips

Even little clovers speak your name
When they turn their faces and smile each morn
As do leaves whispering your I love you's
When the wind speaks its secrets
Softly in my ear

Sun, rain, tiny birds, the horny-toads
Smile whenever you dance into my wonder
The window to my soul gapes wide
To accompany the pleasure that you bring

Now, the man in me only hears
What my little boy could never understand

Hah! Still, even this man of worldly-insight
Cannot fathom what only the vivid consciousness

Behind the Smile!

Of all the universe sees floating
In your spirit's milk

It is then ~ I know I want to be in you
Forever, I want to die in your arms

Until that moment stands astride my manhood
Knowing...
Life has spent all it can allow on me

There is but one goal
One final destination
All that I am

And it is in this ethereally spatial wonder
That I finally must bow down to:

All life's splendor has taught me
All I shall finally glimpse
For after an eternity

It is enough to finally embrace
The understanding that

All I ever wanted or ever could,
Is...
To be your man

(Free Verse)

Upon these words ~

~_____~**~_____~

Beside thee there, I am, My Love,
sure as the stars above all shine.
In each and every gentle breeze
I whisper softly, "You are mine."

Then, everywhere the air's alive,
as 'round your waist my strong arm slips ...
a kiss so tenderly befalls
sweet pomegranate of your lips ...

Against me tight, you feel deep warmth
begin to flow all through your veins ...
inside your core, my beating heart
has come to steal all life's dire pains.

Within these moments, O' My Dear,
this world becomes a better place,
with children's laughter in the air,
a happy smile on every face.

On high above, pure white clouds drift,
softly 'neath cerulean skies ...
as one, our souls begin to sing;
again, that sparkle in your eyes.

Cease thee, ye raging dogs of war,
let's hear enthralling song from birds,
a honey bee on every flow'r,
lifting our hearts ... upon these words ~

~―――――――――~**~―――――――――~

(Quatrains in 8-Count)

When morning calls ~

I wonder...
is it the happy chatter
of early squirrels and birds,
that wakens me;
or, the way you stir inside
that entices the covers
to wrap-up warmly;
clinging affection
embraced 'round willing legs,
half-opened bedroom eyes
imagining it's your arms,
hungered ruby lips;

or, indeed,
could it be that
life, itself, is calling...
its colours,
endless textures
and hues luring me,
enticing me up, into your
warm gentleness...
that tender flow
I've come to recognize,
to feel upon every place,
beneath my all;

Behind the Smile!

secret places
even I dare not go...
places meant only for You,
for your arousing touch
to awaken my fervor,
ignite my essence...
the man in me,
your man?

In such a...
monumental moment,
who could doubt there's God;
for, whom else
could have so perfectly
designed every vibrant cell's fiber,
each thought into feeling
deeply dreamt, each emotion
beneath soft ochre moons
and hot golden suns?

We're constantly blended,
You and I ~
like smooth water's
surface changing to air
without distinct separation,
gradual, a metamorphosis,
one becomes the other;
even each breath,
each heartbeat
and soft sigh
is the same.

Even
trees disrobe,
tempting us recline
beneath them, together
in the joy of endless colour,
soft crackl'ing in playful wonder.

Youthful stirrings recalling
to brisk winter's morns,
when all the world
was contained
in a kiss.

How could
one ever resist
such an invitation,
the deepest compelling
one has ever known or shall?

Yes,
I know well
what it means...
when morning calls ~

———~**~———————

(Free Verse)

SENSUALITY

~ A'wandering with You ~

Many are those times
when I've dreamt in rhymes

we've gone hand-in-hand
wand'ring 'cross the land

there beneath blue skies
a'gaze in your eyes

on soft leaves we laid
whispers softly made

kisses to your hair
sparks of passion flare

soft lips moist and warm
sweet to mine conform

pressing frame to frame
nudges light the flame

feet and legs entwine
ahhh, such feeling's fine

wand'ring hands explore
'tis what wand'ring's for

how we wander so
only we will know.

(Rhyming Couplets)

Sensuality

~ all that I feel....

I've known...
for the longest how far
outside of reality I've always been;
that is, for those claiming
to know its relevance –
the essence of it all.

But, it really makes no difference
because I, also, now know...
yes, I know
what the reality of true love is;
and, guess what?

It's nothing like the romance novels say
or that all the classical poets spout.

There's nothing in type or ink or lead
that comes close
to the feeling I get
that swirls up from my loins
or flips inside my breast
when you say simply,
"I'm yours, my gorgeous man!"

No storm could be more powerful
to what rages inside me
from one of your ethereal

kisses on my neck,
as your lips find their way
onto the circuits of my pulse...
the flow of my river ~
into You.

Oh, I'll readily admit...
clouds have a far better view
of your forest strolls,
of your moments
spent shoveling snow
under the a-gape attention
to your tight hips and
God-graced bosom...
from awed passersby.

But, they don't know either,
when I swim into
the emerald ocean of your eyes,
recall a robin's satin breast, or...
the soft sweetness of a yellow rose,
I'll feel your need boring
into my hungry soul
always and forevermore,
yes, they can't possibly know
~ all that I feel...

~_____~**~_____~

(Free Verse)

BEHIND CLOSED EYES...

Behind closed eyes our deep dreams run,
   and soon we drift off ~ far away...
  Your eyes, my shadow veils from sun,
    around your face soft tresses play.

   So warm my touch there against You,
    we lie 'longside clear silver streams.
    Drift slowly by, white clouds on blue,
    'pon lush, green grass we share our dreams.

    You feel soft kisses brush your face,
    so close my breath, you're breathing-in.
    Your fingers trace my rigid grace,
    wet kisses roam your silk-smooth skin.

    Warm lips caress soft quiv'ring thighs,
   and there upon our grassy bed,
  colours explode behind our eyes,
  as clouds blush down from overhead.

 Love there transcends all time and space,
  and sets two souls as one a'glow.
 Contentment rests upon each face...
eyes op'ning wide ~ we smile and know.

(Parabolic Quatrains)

Betwixt Your Charms ~

—————~**~—————

Last night I wandered out beside the pond
to spend some time with you the way I do.
'Twas then a warmness joined us in a bond
I can't deny sweet yearnings had bade true.

I swear ~ upon my cheek I felt your touch;
it seemed from gentle stars your hands were made,
and sparklings falling from them floated such
that in my eyes soft, tender dreamlight played.

Your breath within my heart was all I heard,
except the vibrant echoes of all time
alive inside that spoke without a word,
transporting us into a world sublime.

I closed my eyes, you flew into my arms,
and took me then 'n there ~ betwixt your charms.

—————~**~—————

(English Sonnet)

Close soft thine eyes ~*
_____~**~_____~

So many moons have passed and gone,
but never so our love divine;
through passing years we've carried-on,
such is the fate when souls entwine.

Vows laid upon our yellow rose
were made and never have they waned;
nor, shall cold shadows e'er impose,
or dim this flame that God's ordained.

Here, by my side, through thick and thin,
thy held mine hand and lit the path,
that I may never know chagrin;
nor, cleave made whole ... once more in half.

Each gentle wind whispers thy name,
each firefly's glow spiels my heartbeat,
sweet drops of wine, each like your flame,
that sates my thirst for life replete.

Thy labored breath a'blend with mine,
in such a way with harmony ...
sensations undulate divine,
soaking our nights in ecstasy.

Behind the Smile!

Will e'er I kiss thy glist'ning rose?
If only in my dreams thou taste
befalls our passion's fire ~ that ever grows,
thine honeyed drips 'pon my tongue placed ...

close soft thine eyes and know I'm there
'pon every place and all within;
then, feel my flames throughout thee flare,
each licking flick ~ hot sparks begin.

Whilst even now my passions thrust
deep ~ from thy charms they're driven fore,
'tis not but power of pure lust,
yet, love that burns forevermore.

Oh, carry me to thou, Sweetheart,
entwine me in thine warmth's embrace,
that nevermore our frames will part;
nor, from my heart ~ thy loving face.

Forget not e'er that night we met,
how all at once we knew our fate,
with each new touch, gold type was set,
in language ~ only We translate*

———————~**~———————————~

(Quatrains in 8-Count)

Divine Treasures ~

That day he felt your sunshine all throughout
the pleasures of this young boy's heart were filled,
he wanted nothing, but to run and shout ...
his yearnings for you never would be stilled.

He loved God's flowers, more than words can tell,
but never near as much as your bouquet.
Your warm, moist lips made more than his heart swell,
while joining with you took his breath away.

The rise and fall of every motions' wave,
were mirrored in each thrust of passion's throes;
so beautiful ... the sating that you gave
was answered ~ perfect pulsing of thy rose.

The ache he'd felt, now sated for awhile,
your divine treasures ~ bade a grateful smile.

(English Sonnet)

E'er gently eternal ~

Last night, beside me
there you lay,
across the bed
in disarray.

I'd kissed your lips,
I must confess ...
slipped-in beneath
thy evening dress.

In passion's quest,
such beauty fair,
caressed your breasts
with tender care.

Imploring eyes
smiled up at me,
whisp'ring my name ...
"I'm yours, feel free."

My heart, it sighed,
nightingales sang,
as all around
love's wind-chimes rang.

Sensuality

Still, when the morn
opened mine eyes,
remained sweet splendor
of thy thighs.

Stirring, I stretched
with arms spread wide ...
your beguiling voice,
e'er gently ~ deep inside.

Whence took that world
where love-light streams
those fields of golden daffodils,
we strolled in lover's lofty dreams?

Now, as I write, my olde pen smiles,
ink flowing gold and free ...
pondering how when we met,
your sweet love first touched me.

(Unmetered Quatrains)

Endless Life

The rising sun, cool morning dew,
    leaves dance upon soft breeze.
In all the world around lives You;
    soft glows your colors' ease.

Slip into slacks 'n sandals, too;
    shirtless, I take a walk.
Each step I take, a step for two,
    our hearts in silent talk.

Stroll we along in loving grace
    'til all our cares have flown;
tender the light to match thy face,
    your touch ignites my own.

Then, leaning back you pull me down
    atop ~ between warm thighs,
the universe soaring around,
    all life shared in our eyes.

Beneath their treetop homes we lie,
    God's birds and creatures play.
Above it all, a clear blue sky ...
    we have our blissful way.

Our kisses breathe all we've longed for,
each breath a lifetime's sigh,
as fauna silently adore ~
in harmony our cry.

Then, happily they sing along,
we rest there wrapped-up tight,
while hum two souls life's endless song,
clinging with all our might.

In us, all time has ceased to turn,
the world and all its strife;
never more deep will passions burn,
You are my endless life ~

―――――~**~―――――

(Ballad)

Femme Coquette ...

Her voice bit into him like lacquered nails
that screeched across the blackboard of his mind;
as cold as rime, she's thin as ice that fails,
and is so dark she leaves the senses blind.

She emptied him and stole away his peace ...
left naught behind but grief-filled memory.
For those of you who might this wailing cease,
judge not too harshly what you cannot see;

that once a man is softened in his heart
to trusting in a hardened femme coquette,
there is no way to stop before the start
of all to come that he'll not soon forget.

Her heat set high his lust to blazing fire,
then left his ashes on her cold stone pyre.

(English Sonnet)

...—~•:* God's Paintbrush 'n Palette *:•~—...
~ Chosen and Blessed ~

.~:*:~.

From the pomegranate..
The warm pink rose..
Flame of passion's desire..
He brushed your cheeks,
Our tongues and lips,
Inside your sweet cathedral,
The head of my spire,
Each to fit like fine pieces
of an intricate puzzle..

.~:*:~.

Yes, He mated us perfectly.

From the highest skies,
The fragrant flowers..
The deepest sea..
He mixed His colors,
He stroked his mighty brush,
Upon the canvas of my life,
The windows to Your soul,
That I climbed into,
Like a hungry burglar..

.~:*:~.

Your boundless emerald eyes..

Behind the Smile!

From the sun..
The finest gold from
deep within the earth..
The harvest moon..
China's finest silk..
He spread His colors,
A crown to adorn your head,
Aroma of sweet oils,
Set my amazed eyes aglow,
Inviting my strong fingers into..
.~:*:~.
Your golden, flowing mane.

From the reaping..
The ripest melons..
Topaz stems, my
tongue and teeth to taste..
He harvested life's milk,
To grace my chest,
Sublimely my caress,
Beckon my lips to savor..
.~:*:~.
Your supple, glorious breasts.

Upon His pallet..
He blended the finest
of satin, ivory and cream..
Soft and smooth as gossamer wing,

Sensuality

Fashioned over your lustrous frame,
Against my rough skin,
My urgent hands to seek,
The textures of heaven,
That I might come to know..
.~:*:~.
Your blissfully heaven-kissed skin.

Finally, from the stars..
The universe of love..
From all the wisdom
great minds ardently seek..
He mixed a medium rare,
Into lovely stardust splendor,
Sprinkled it upon his pallet,
Endless colors, hues, and tints,
His eternally-endless textures,
That I might gaze upon,
The greatest masterpiece,
The world has ever known..
.~:*:~.
His greatest eternally-enthralling miracle,
He so wondrously crafted into..
.~:*YOU*:~.
.~:*:~.
•
.

(Free Verse)

Behind the Smile!

Golden Crown
~.•.~**~.•.~

Delicately smooth ~
as cornsilk's satin sheen
gently yields unto the touch.

~.•.~.•.~.•.~.•.~.•.~

Your smile,
sweet breath,
your whispers,
creamy moisture
'pon my manly hand,
the inner of your thighs,
enchantment in your eyes,
stirs these aching loins to rise.
Through the window of my soul,
your drifting essence makes me whole.

~.•.~.•.~.•.~.•.~**~.•.~.•.~.•.~.•.~

Brightly across the landscapes in my mind,
of You, wondrous eternal images unwind.
Your graceful feet ... toes playfully tease,
it is Me, only You know how to please.
Soft on the breeze a leaf drifts down,
reflects in sunlight, golden brown;
and, everywhere the soul can see,
your face appears enchantingly.
Send down, yon stars above,
truly to me, my only love.
For, now the moonlight
set passion to flight,
while all around,
n'er a sound,
save nigh,
a sigh!
Upon my shoulder
your head lies gently down.
Our wine, as it grows sweetly older,
and life and love turns to a golden crown.

~.•.~.•.~.•.~.•.~**~.•.~.•.~.•.~.•.~

(Concrete)

Heart to Heart

Locked in love's gaze, our eyes ablaze,
lips yearning to be kissed ...
waves of pleasure grow in measure
we know we can't resist.

Your whispers soft, I soar aloft,
we feel life's pulsing beat ...
Our bodies touch, it is too much,
we can't resist the heat.

I lay you down, I want to drown
myself in You tonight ...
between our thighs a thrumming rise;
oh, how it feels just right!

Our lips touch warm, all through us swarm
sensations hunger knows ...
and from each kiss, we can't dismiss
the aching urge that grows.

Dear, hold me tight, with all your might,
we sense what will take place ...
warm, wet - you're lush, still I won't rush,
but savour slow your grace.

Sweet, pulsing mound, my digits found
soft touching stokes pure heat …
it's off we go, love's rivers flow,
two hearts to Nature's beat.

Our world a'spin, I'm ent'ring in,
engulfed by passion's fire …
I want to flow, to let it go,
deluge of hot desire.

The moment's nigh, love's soaring high,
'twas destined from the start …
through every phase, love's flame ablaze,
souls touching ~ heart to heart.

―――――――――~**~―――――――――

(Eights 'n Sixes)

Sensuality

How it used to be...

I thought of You
and all time stood still,
the winds of primal urge
swept me away,
away unto your,
aching limbs.

A voice,
a whisper really,
soft, warm,
urging my senses
to give-way,
surrendering to
my own yearning,
for our passions ...
your warmth,
your sweet, full lips
upon me.

It was then I knew,
what had always been
will always be,
and at every moonrise,
I'd feel your thighs,

Behind the Smile!

gaze into your
verdant eyes,
listen to
your willing sighs.

You ~
my hungered prize,
your perfect size ...
the fit that's
always pleased.

Come!
Show me how
to make love again,
seems I recall,
but want you now,
and I ache ...
for how it used to be.

(Free Style)

In Such Dreams ~

You stood right here before me, Dear ...
shone with the brightest glow,
I was aware that everywhere
our world began to slow.

This timeless space became your grace ...
it was right then I knew;
life sparkled fine, like ancient wine,
each sip a taste of You.

Lips softly meet, such flavors sweet,
the universe our world ...
in every place I saw your face,
my senses all unfurled.

You smelled of spice, like paradise ...
when we touched, hot sparks flew;
'twas then we kissed, a gentle mist
of stardust's golden hue

fell all around ... there was no sound,
except your tender sighs.
You took my hand, then bade me stand,
looked deep into my eyes:

Behind the Smile!

A gentle stroke – each word you spoke,
calmed down my every fear ...
with much in-store, I wanted more,
down your cheek rolled a tear.

With care I asked, "Has sorrow passed?"
You smiled and touched my face;
"No, my sweet man, it has began,"
took me in warm embrace,

"as passions grow, my rivers flow,
alluring you to me;
aching pure bliss, I crave your kiss ...
yearn our sweet ecstasy."

Your hem lifted, I was gifted,
when you laid me down.
The spell then broke when I awoke,
"Ahhh, in such dreams I'd drown."

~_____~**~_____~

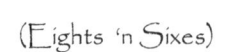

~·~·~...IN THESE QUIET PLACES...~·~·~

Come, let me softly pull you into our quietness
where wonder has etched the loveliness of
your alluring, luscious emerald eyes
permanently into my hopeful,
azure blues,
where the dawns rise silently ~ gently
to mist our early skies with gold
before surrendering...
on unto the day.

Let us entwine our ever-willing, hungry fingers
in quiet, reverent solitude...
to stroll through boundless amber fields,
where the stalks of wheat in training
learn to weather life's gloriously
gentled breath of creation,
waving as one together
at all awe-struck
passers-by.

Let me know you in your quiet stillness,
as I have known you like soft waves
fondling the excited shore, while
You are siren, I am sailor...
where the all of us is
~ Eternity.

Let me love you in your calm moments,
that I may know it is me your loins
open in aching hunger for, and
it is for me your eyes close
when your sighs breathe
and flow softly down
o'er me from your
lusty throat.

Then, in the solitude of this time, Our time...
embraced in these hushed surroundings,
let our souls meld into matrimony,
with no clergy or witnesses,
....and....
in these quiet places, let me be
the sole reason your arms,
your moist lips, and
your world
exists.

(Free Verse)

~ Real love have I ~

These stars a'twinkle in my eyes
so soft, are only yours;
reflected universe of love
out from my heart it pours;

Lust's river's warmth I flow through thee
in full each rill to sate.
for current's force You've opened wide,
bourn my hard urging's weight.

Our dreams' sweet shared imaginings
enfolding life's embrace
worlds in our hearts to anywhere,
no others fill our space.

The ways you've spoilt me like a king
upon his lofty throne,
Ours, the only real love have I ~
or shall have ever known.

(Unmetered Quatrains)

Secret Rendezvous

You smile at me
I smile at thee
and all the air's a'fire.
You touch me there,
I do declare,
Such bliss you so inspire!

What shall we do
I'm asking you,
is there a place to go?
Secrets we'll share
while we're in there...
and no one else will know.

(Quickie)

Speak to Me ~

Oh, speak to me in words that stoke my fires,
those aches inside no other's voice inspires.

In moments clear, with words I understand;
embrace me in hot rhythms un-preplanned.

Yes, speak to me in ways I've never known;
sweet senses high, all of your passions grown.

Then, show me what it's like I'm so adored,
there is no place your lips have not explored.

Come soft, caress my cheek and whisper low;
then, hold me warm and close that I will know,

there is no one or place for me on Earth
who touches deeper or with greater mirth,

those special spots I know no other can ...
it's in this way I'll always ~ be your man.

(Rhyming Couplets)

Sweetheart

Some lonely night, your heart takes flight,
a warmth pulses down there.
Remember Sweet, you are my treat;
and, I'm your man to share.

I'll taste your lips, embrace your hips
with passion you will love.
This gentle man with tender hand
like a soft satin glove,

will soothe your fears, quell all sad tears,
hold closely all night long.
Comes nigh daybreak, I'll for your sake
sing sweetly our love's song.

Come to me now, let me endow
all me I have to give.
Don't hesitate, ere it's too late
come share all we can live.

"Babe" you call me, sweet melody,
your sensual lush charms.
Stirrings I feel, wondrously real,
Sweetheart, there in your arms.

(Eights 'n Sixes)

"Tears of yesterday's longing..."

Tears of yesterday's longing flow
like warm, silver rivers bestow
to the seas that nurture our lives...
that which lovers need feel.
Knowing swift flows of ecstasy,
the heat flash touch of you to me,
bring rushing carnal waves of bliss;
a want I can't conceal.

Tears of yesterday's longing flow
drip softly down to make me grow;
like roses parched crave gentle rain,
with thirsts quenched, blush anew.
Touch each, my teardrops, as they fall,
taste their sweet sparkling, one and all,
release your honeyed gush o'er me...
ne'er bitter tears for you.

No tears of yesterday's longing...
sense only our deep belonging,
and ne'er here-fore feel saddened pain,
because I am your love.
Can you not feel and can't you see
the joy that moves inside of me...
all that makes me, thirsty for you?
Cleansing tears ~ from above.

(Spilling Ink)

Behind the Smile!

Tell it to the ochre moon.....!
...a bit long, I think, for some, but you may like it...

Just one more sleepless night wondering ...
where you might be, if I'm there with you
in your lonely arms, under your heated frame
to sate your need of me, of us?

Though, I know my thoughts are as thin as air
and my dreams are in there, too;
somehow, being inhaled by every breath taken,
always the flavor of You
upon this thirsting tongue.

So, the ebon cool of Mother Nature
called me out again,
to visit her twinkling, multi-colored,
diamond stars once more ...
to share in the homage of your name and soul,
she always gifts me in her breeze.

Strange ...
I never really considered how
cold wind could feel so warm until now,
and I must have felt it at least ...
let me see; a thousand times.

Then, it dawned on me ...
she's telling me from the inside-out.

Again ... wondering why I never felt
how coldness can seem so warm?
Guess it's always been good enough
to just have you ... think I'll go back to that.

You know?
I just now noticed ...
the pond is lit by a full moon,
the color of your thrilling golden mane.

Even stars are sparkling
Emerald and azure tonight,
the willow sighing, rubbing its leaves,
softly whispering, "I love you, my man,"
and I swore I heard a cricket 'neath my chair ...
in a low chirp ... speak your name over and again.

About then I began to speak,
and all became quiet, save for my lonely voice ...
not lonely in the usual sense,
but with honor and love,
respect and awe ... loving, caring reverence,
the way only captured hearts can.

Behind the Smile!

Yes, I spoke alright ...
with moments recalled when we laughed,
when we made ardent love over the miles,
the oceans, the mountains, the cooing doves,
beds of pink carnations and hibiscus ~
those times you cried at my songs for you ...
I from your sweet, tender need of me.

Oh, I had lots to say, alright,
and you can believe I said it all ...
while my little world listened,
yes, quietly, reverently almost ...
not daring interrupt the moment shared;
our moment ~ one more ethereal,
one more heavenly time.

After-all ...
how often is it that frogs and sleepy turtles,
the spirits of my loyal departed little friends
(each buried with love and gentle care
out here beside the pond),
and Mother Nature, Herself,
have the opportunity to be awoken,
to hear the voice of human love ~
spoken with such fervor?

Well, you can bet I looked around ...
just to make sure no human
was sharing our private solitude,
because I know how much you seem to care.

So, my Beloved Woman,
look up tonight into the ebon sky ...
and as those twinkling emerald-azure stars
reflect in your eyes,
listen closely and you will hear, too;

because, I'm there ...
even the tiniest sigh this heart,
this soul of mine, yours, too, could breath,
it's then, you'll hear and know ... because,
all is shared with You when I ~
tell it to the ochre moon....!

(Free Verse)

~ We Soar, We Dream Forevermore ~
~ our wings ~

~˜.•*•.˜~

When nighttime calls silk shadows fall~
Soaring into my dreams you lay onto me,
With opened arms bestow to you my all~
Flowing grace smoothly I throughout thee.

~=*=~

Can you feel me growing there love true~
Penetrate deeply into your sweetest soul?
Ne'er inhaling e'er life's breath from you~
Now, but this man's inspired, eternal goal.

~=*=~

Where once darkness fell upon this path~
Many times there I stumbled, where I'd fell,
Softly aglow we shared my bed.. my bath~
Soaring now into your lovely caring spell.

~=*=~

Sensuality

.
_=*=_
.

Your hands alive in this moment caressing deep~
Glide softly my sea, lay upon this hungry shore,
You come to dwell ... to love me within this sleep~
Entwined are we in the embrace of passion's arms

.
_=*=_
.

We soar,
We dream,
"Forevermore"

.
~~.•*•.~~
*

(Unmetered Quatrains w/Envoy)

~ on lovely wings of gold, My Love ~
"....this one speaks for itself...."

~ Wild flames of dreams ~

I knew I should have dressed accordingly
to fight ache's rush of dreams off in the night;
had I pre-known the heat consuming me,
I'd lain me down in naught but soft moonlight.

Oft, too, when nighttime calls, there comes a yawn;
then, one cannot foresee what dreams will bring ...
a melody through realms twixt dusk and dawn,
we hear those songs that only souls can sing.

Ethereal in-time merge passions fleet,
to quickened rhythms' rocking in the night,
whilst warm their pearl-lit rivers' flowing beat,
embraced, two lovers cling with all their might.

Tho, in wild flames of dreams we may succumb,
too seldom dreams ~ realities become.

(English Sonnet)

Woman's Touch

Pon me I feel your woman's touch
that ever thrills my heart so much.

Then, sweeps a warm and gentle breeze,
whispering softly thru the trees,

high from blue skies and all around
sighs such a wonderful, sweet sound.

Now, all our world is set aglow,
as liquid love begins to flow ...

searing hot passion's rising fire
surge swiftly up my rigid spire.

Such pleasures in us we have grown,
a gift two lovers can't postpone.

(Rhyming Couplets)

Behind the Smile!

"Your Sweet Rain"

Unquenched, my thirst cries out for your sweet rain,
for there's no other's whom shall sate this thirst.
Ope wide thy gate that I may drink again ...
I crave from thee warm sips thou hath coerced.
With thine sweet rain fill me until I burst ~
Moon, down in all your glory, shine o'er us ...
pearl-glinted waves a'flow merge two as one
these souls to e'er be bound with golden truss;
soft, tender ties by loving hands were spun,
and nevermore they're e'er to be undone.

Strike, Eros, love's air in torrid flash;
stir dark clouds, a most ferocious storm,
send your winds in taunted, howling clash ...
then, command all elements conform,
that, we'll breathe your sultry atmosphere;
moist, as dewdrops sweet upon the tongue,
like a taste from joyous saline tear,
or the silken flow lovemaking's sprung.
Sing the songs of rain 'til they're all sung.

Sensuality

// " //
O' how I've dreamt and yearned your taste
I lack tempest words to tell it.
Never's been known such a sad waste
and there's nothing can dispel it,
but to receive my fill of you ...
to sate this ever-thirsting pit,
all from a spell I must pursue
by every ploy within my wit.
` , . '
Come, show me your oasis ~
un-parch my thirst ~ at your well.
Fill all my empty spaces,
and release this arid spell.
Let me partake thy graces,
where I ever long to dwell
as I feel my ardor swell.
// ' / ·
To quell a man's dire need,
a wondrous thing to do;
for, always he'll concede
his loyalty to you.
With pitcher filled to brim
give all you have to him.
'/'·// ' /// /
No better way known
do I have to say,

Behind the Smile!

"If your man has flown,
bring him back to stay,
and ever atone
// " ♪ //
with your dear ways
that he will know
for all his days
you love him so!"
♪ / ' ♪ / .
Lover's task;
You, I ask,
"Fill my flask!"
♪ / ` / / / ♪
Champagne
refrain ...
` , ` '
"Rain!"
/ / / / / " ♪ / / / / / / / / / / /
♪ , ` ♪ ` ♪ ` ♪

(Diminished Pentaverse)

FANTASY

An Angel's Love ~

Across my fields of wonder ... drifting by,
like ribbons floating through a wispy dream,
a nymphette whispered soft my name ~ a sigh;
'twas there she stood inside a golden beam.

Her verdant eyes shined like a polished gem,
with sparkling glints that hypnotized my soul,
and (somehow) I was drawn deep into them
in such a way I knew I'd been made whole.

Faint sounds of crystal waters dancing by,
on velvet mossy banks she lay me down.
She taught me love there 'neath that azure sky,
then wrapped us warm inside her pure white gown.

She took my breath and breathed it back in me;
that instant knew ~ she'd set my spirit free.

(English Sonnet)

Daydreaming's Gifts

With morning tea, wafts a spell
my wandering mind must tell,
of fairest moments sharing Her today.

Crystal pond, wave cattails tall,
of life's joys, I've known most all;
yet, to Her sunny smile my daydreams stray.

Vividly ... lush, tender lips,
«come, take me» eyes, steamy sips
I dream will lead us into passion's play.

Soft, aglow ... like gleaming gold,
tend›rest of life›s gifts unfold;
in every sip I taste her sweet bouquet.

(Primetime)

Dream Lovers ~

This hand feel brush softly thy cheek,
these lips moist on thy own,
our breathing's quickened, gazing deep,
with passion's fingers' moan.

To thee I cannot voice these words
lived deep within my heart,
for never have I felt before
sensations dreams impart.

Know that we shall forever be,
our love can never die,
from dusk 'til dawn in love entwined
dreams flamed by passions high.

Dwells ever, these imaginings;
alive, sweet ardent schemes,
waiting that time e'er we shall meet
we'll flow as one in dreams.

'Til then we'll keep on dreaming dreams
our fantasies implore;
who knows, one day may come we two
will have to dream no more.

(Ballad)

~ Dreams in Flight ~

What was it swept so softly through the night,
imploring sweetness through my dreams,
and was it really as it seems;
or, could it be but passion's yearning flight?

Outside, there waves the willow an invite
and hosts the nightbird's luring song;
a melody known all along,
sweet thrumming tones in tune with pure delight.

Was it, I wonder, wrought by pale moonlight,
beneath its silv'ry, glowing beams,
in liquid ribbons' living streams ~
or, gentle spark'lings in your eyes so bright?

(Tenz 'n Eightz)

Eden's Haven...

There is a place I long to be,
to sit and dream awhile ...
where gently calls to me your voice
from many a far mile.

A place where spark'ling di'mond glints
play with dancing ripples,
relenting to soft moonlit night's
undulating dimples.

'Tis peaceful there without a care,
a haven wrought by fate ...
and everywhere a song of life
to fill us and elate.

Oh, grip us tight, Eternity,
embrace with no more stress;
an Eden built by dreams for two ...
all mine – I must confess.

(Ballad)

Fantasy

Green Eyes ~

Eastward ~ my ship's bound 'pon this night
I'm standing at the rail,
stars in the skies, o' guide me right
this voyage must not fail.
Many the times I've dreamt of thee
beside You on your land,
t'ward morning's sun 'cross silver sea
I sail to take thy hand.
O' fairest of the fair so blessed
for whom this heart beats long,
the soul of me shall never rest
'til we're a single song.
Like sparkling of the krill a'dance
spilled over by the prow,
Green Eyes, I'm captive in thy trance
enthralled, I do avow.
O' land me there upon thine shore
taste mine lips, thou wonder,
may your sweet charms forevermore
ne'er be set asunder.
And, when each Spring bequeaths new life,
our bond we will renew;
turned into bliss, life freed from strife
I'll e'er, Green Eyes, love You ~

(Ballad)

...I Am...

I am the snow, the light and wind,
the ice-glazed wonder
of the trees ...

the comfy blanket soft and warm,
soft dove nestled in its leaves.
A wind-chime's dance
enchanting thee,

the lace upon your windowpane,
love song's flowing melody,
the beat of your heart
in every breath
you take;

Most of all,
I am in your soul and spirit,
as you are alive in mine
and all things free
in my world.

Yes, I am forever You,
as You are Me.

(Free Style)

Ode to Vivid Dreams ~*

Last night, I chatted with a dear-heart friend,
we had not spoken for awhile, you know;
it's odd how time can suddenly transcend,
seems only yesterday I'd felt her glow.

Sometimes, some things keep warmest in the heart;
what better place for treasures could there be?
I knew at once I loved her from the start ...
yet, from afar stretched-out our destiny.

Tonight I dreamt of silky, golden hair ~
a woman's warmth caressed my every place;
with eyes as green as grass, her skin so faire,
with goddess' smile, God's gifted angel face.

At morn, warm sunbeams climbed up 'cross the bed;
soft, in my arms ~ lay cradled her sweet head.

(English Sonnet)

...ROBBIE...

His tungsten frame and shell buffed gleaming bright,
sharp positronic brain with laser eyes,
each pinioned joint was smoothly torqued just right;
'twas said that Robbie is the perfect size,

to fit in every way in every place,
a robot needs to do that fills his tasks;
each wiring circuit made to interface,
so he'd perform what anyone should ask.

They were surprised about the heart he grew;
"It was a miracle!" is what they said.
When Robbie met the lovely robot, Soo –
It's then their polished chrome turned scarlet red.

Who could have thought two robots of their kind
might ever meet, and true love they would find?

(English Sonnet)

~·~Recalling the Sky~·~

Through forests deep ... far past meand'ring glen,
    a wolf roams (in his heart) beside the sea.
With softened gaze, out there where dreams begin,
    it was the brush of feathered soul that he
had felt, and knew it drew him back within ...
    intense, on high, when yearning wings soared free.
In endless dreams he knew he'd too long been
    entombed, and, like the prisoner, must flee;

    a soul unsheathed from wild and furry frame,
    to be again ~ that gull he'd once became.

(Ottava Rima)

. . . save You!

There You sat ...
beside the pond,
tanned dancer's toes
dangling,
teasing,
as if to invite,
"Explore me!"

A breath-stealing surprise
like none before,
beautifully, your hair tousled
in the wind,
kissed golden by the sun ...

your flashing apple-green eyes,
and all I could manage
was to sigh
and marvel,
dumfounded ... stunned
as lazy, dappled shadows
shed by watchful willows
danced back and forth
across the grass,
entrancing shape of
your sheer gown and arm,

Fantasy

*sparkling ripples,
how shy, rustling cattails
spoke softly ...
with all the allure they could muster,*

*and so much more
of Nature
stole me away ...
though, they did not realize
they all futilely
were competing
with splendor the likes
God blessed on nothing else,
... save You!*

(Free Verse)

Sweet Island Girl ~

As she pulls back her flaxen, sun-kissed hair,
in golden ink 'pon parchment life is spilt ...
a tender goddess dwells within warmth's care,
inside a world of words emotions built.

With eyes so green, in them one could get lost,
she gazes into those that call her name.
Like magic, words of light are softly tossed
by hands of God's pure glory in acclaim.

Imbue us with your splendor, O' divine...
Sweet Island Girl ~ tan skin so softly-kissed
by tropic's rays caressed, so sweetly thine,
your ocean charms no heart could e'er resist.

Intoxicate with Virgin Isle champagne ...
Sweet Island Girl ~ flow o'er us love's refrain!

(English Sonnet)

Fantasy

To vivid dreams ∼

I spoke awhile with a dear-hearted friend,
   we had not chatted for awhile, you know;
it's odd how time can suddenly transcend,
   seems only yesterday I'd felt her glow.
Sometimes, some things keep warmest in the heart;
   what better place for treasures could there be?
I knew at once I loved her from the start ...
   yet, from afar stretched-out our destiny.
Last night I dreamt of silky, golden hair ∼
   a woman's warmth caressed my every place;
soft eyes as green as grass, with skin so faire,
   her smile lit-up a pure, angelic face.

At morn, soft sunbeams climbed up 'cross the bed;
   there, in my arms, lay cradled her sweet head.

(English Sonnet)

~ When I hear your call ~

Raindrops fell soft on my roof last night,
dripped silv'ry glints down off the eave;
no stars shined out with all their might,
moonbeams fell dark in quiet reprieve;

peace, feather-soft throughout my core,
quick tempo'd drip with each heartbeat,
aye felt your breath's touch gentle more
held deep within our dreams e'er sweet.

Fluffed robins perch'd upon their roosts,
where oft they wait in rain burst's gush;
squirrel tails a'flick and chatters loosed,
while you dwell warm inside my hush.

Such moments many, where once few,
e'er 'fore I'd heard your footsteps fall.
So, come on storms and pour anew,
it's sunny when I hear your call ~

(Quatrains in 8-Count)

...when you walk with me...

in flowers' home
our footsteps
languidly fall side by side
shuffling slowly
to life's song
to our hearts' beat

then, I thought...
why is it
when your skirt
floats up
between your slender legs
I can hear the wind
call me to look

hmm

odd that I would
question God's directive
the way ...
your hair flirts
with my amazement
the way bees find honey
I find yours

is it
I wonder ...

Behind the Smile!

laughter of
children on a swing
the way a cloud
fills the sky
or how a bird
knows its mate instantly
that draws me
into you

telling me how lucky I am
like
those ageless stones
beneath your feet
touched
over and over again
in such
tenderness

as you do
each and every time
when You walk with me?

(Free Verse)

Fantasy

WOODSPRITE—————————~*

Whilst wand'ring through the woods one sunny day,
came I upon a sprite so wondrous faire ...
she danced ~ then, whirled and stole my heart away.

Oh, how the air became so light and gay ...
each sunbeam glinting through her golden hair,
whilst wand'ring through the woods one sunny day.

'Twas once her hand brushed mine in gleeful play,
with tenderness and loving, gentle care
she danced ~ then, whirled and stole my heart away.

That instant...yes, my world began to sway;
I fell in-love with her right then and there,
whilst wand'ring through the woods one sunny day.

The atmosphere turned sweet with rose bouquet;
as symphonies of birdsong filled the air ~
she danced ~ then, whirled and stole my heart away.

Again a youth, my hair no longer grey ...
'tis truth I speak to you, I do declare:
Whilst wand'ring through the woods one sunny day,
she danced ~ then, whirled and stole my heart away.

(Villanelle)

You ~

I wonder if you think of me
(not that I deserve you to),
of how softly love's flowed free
straight from my heart right into you.

A songbird stopped-by on the limb
close there beside my windowpane.
Its song was but a tiny chirp;
yet, made my heart whisper your name.

Sunshine's rays through dappled leaves
and children's laughter filled the air,
a sort of gentleness touched me ...
for sure I knew that you'd been there.

It may just be a trick of mind
or that which happens rare in time,
but on my oath I swear it's true,
for naught, save You ~ feels this sublime.

(Unmetered Quatrains)

`;.•:*~ You Awaken My Dreams ~*:•.;`

―――――~**~―――――

Word by word
You form before me a golden glow ~
sparkling eyes,
velvet soft full lips,
cheeks smooth as satin,
framed by sun-kissed waves.
Line by line
You dance before me on the page ~
limbs spread wide,
tanned melon breasts,
partake of me deep again
inside thy life-gifting warmth.
Verse by verse
You stir and awaken the man of me ~
arouse each fiber,
flow tender warmth,
caress mind, heart, soul,
vibrant rain upon parched skin.
Rhythm'd rhyme
You flow through each and every place ~
take me home,
where passions rise,
wrapped 'round my hunger,
awakened, soaked in dreams with thee.

―――――~**~―――――

(Free Verse)

~ You're the One ~

For the longest I've been thinking;
not the usual kind of thought,
but of that which speaks of kindness,
and of the sweetheart I have sought.

In this thinking came a notion ...
seems that my thinking's been all wrong,
and despite my good intentions,
I've just been singing the wrong song!

So, I've composed a brand new verse;
I sure do hope you'll like it, too,
because it came straight from my heart,
all the way ~ over there to You.

Please, my past sour tunes forgive,
accept this new one with a smile;
it's written with a billion stars,
in the sweetest heavenly style.

For ink, I used the golden sun,
then blended-in the stratosphere ...
rainbow's colours for melody,
a dash of rivers, spark'ling clear.

Fantasy

*Angels on high, hearing my hymn,
came down to bless it with a kiss;
then, all around chorused-in birds,
ne'er such a symphony as this.*

*Oh, lifetime love, I've sought and found,
beseech me not all I have done ...
there is no other fills my heart,
this song of love sings, "You're the One."*

(Quatrains in 8-Count)

THINKING

A SIMPLE THOUGHT ON UNITY
~ to blending ~

There is "emotion",
there is "education",
there is a way of "feeling" things.

I am all three,
you are all three,
they are all three,
we are all – all three.

I have seen them in each of us ...

I am "I",
I am "you",
I am "they",
I am "we".

Then, are we not all, also, each other?
Do we not cry with hurt the same tears as with joy;
although, with opposite feeling?

Feeling is the one quality that beckons within us all
and makes us one, whether we are aware of it – or not.

If we should not know it,
it means we have no conscious attachment
within our souls,
not that we are separate in our feelings
or in our beings.

So, judge me not, lest ye judge yourself
at the precise moment ...
as, we are surely one,

... You and I ...

(Free Verse)

"Only in our sleeping state of mentality are we separate entities,
while in the conscious mind it is known we are like water and air:
Where one ends the other begins, but not divisively;
for, one blends gradually into the other ~
as does dusk to dawn, dawn to dusk"

AFTERLIFE~~~~~~~~~~~~*

Before a veil, we stand upon this earth,
where none who breathes may see what lies beyond;
perhaps, a place we come from at our birth;
who claims to know, with "truth" cannot respond.

Deep faith is what is carried in each heart
of those whose minds are deep enough to ask,
and once a loved-one's chosen, they depart;
the veil's then lifted from them like a mask.

Fond memories for us they've left behind,
embrace and heal the wounds when they are gone.
It's in this way are kept life's ties that bind, when trav'ling on into
their brand new dawn.

A Mother's gift, the son that she conceives;
God makes her child His own ~ soon as he leaves.

(English Sonnet)

Better things to do ...

I felt it fall upon my hand,
a teardrop soft and warm;
not the usual salty tear,
it fell there to inform:

I'd been remiss (a time or two)
lost in my own concerns,
when every now-n-then a hint,
"Somewhere, a sad heart yearns,"

came on the wind to touch my soul;
I barely noticed it,
and went my way all self-concerned
... quite shallow – I admit.

"I've better things to do," I thought,
"than turn away from me.
Each silly tear that comes my way,
how crucial can it be?

Let each one handle all their own,
no one to dry my eyes,
nor soothe the hurtful things I feel,
the pain that I disguise.

Behind the Smile!

Where is the gentleness so yearned,
for me who aches each night,
and who will come to kiss my lips,
embrace away my fright?"

Somewhere, outside my shadowland
there spoke an angel's voice,
"Please, heed my words, for in them lives
your answer ~ Love's the choice!"

It's then I knew I'd always known
from what source comes such fear,
that every time wet warmth is felt,
it is but my own tear.

(Ballad)

...•CONtroVERsiAL • mE•...

"or, why I seem to be at odds with everyone!"

Pessimists will see
a glass half
empty.

v

~-~-~-~-~-~-~-~-~-~-~-~

^

Optimists
brightly deem
the glass half full.

... while ...

I perceive that
it's just
too

T
A
L
L

(Free Verse)

-= CONSCIOUSNESS =-

~ awakening ~

Alone, on the threshold of new life I stand,
whence can only be glimpsed a distant shore,
growing ever steadily closer now,
while never existing to me before.

~*~

And, that which had become truth to me
Can remain that same truth no longer,
As newly emerging worlds of light
Begin to glow within me ever-stronger.

(Free Verse)

Consciousness begins to form:
"the first moment a mind first grasps there is more, Much More, beyond the world we live in, and that the human world in which we exist is less than a spark in the night amidst the immensity of it all!"

• DESIREE •

—~ a telling ~—

—~—

Diminish self-grown fears
If the thought of leaving makes you cry,
Know only "that" will live forever
Which can never die.

—~—

Windy nights are born
To whisk the light away,
Hands left holding darkness
To touch you in the day.

—~—

Exposing those parts of you
No other eyes have found,
Except the ones of feeling
That give your inner-self the sound.

—~—

As soft as the whisper of silence
Upon the face of a falling leaf,
Within the realms of fantasy
Or some long-ago belief.

—~—

.—~—.

Bringing awareness to travel through
Your mind's fondest schemes,
Asking why what's found
Isn't what it seems.

.—~—.

No need to heed life's lessons
Nor to hear the call,
Trace out your own design
Not the patterns on some wall.

.—~—.

Life's secrets live not in our answers
Nor contained in old-folks' fears,
But within the shattering of life
Told by forlorn lovers' tears.

(Unmetered Quatrains)

~ When minds wander-off ~
".-= we may search for answers in many ways in many places,
but only by living can we truly know =-."

ENIGMA

Upon the road, we look both ways;
such wonders to behold.
What came before and lies ahead
is said to be foretold.

When gazing back at times long past,
some great, some not so good;
each thought is turned to lessons learned,
more clearly understood.

Then, glancing fore – t'ward that to come,
the vision ends quite near;
not yet revealed what shall be found,
beyond that veil so sheer.

With earnest hope and smiles intact,
on each day we embark;
by faith we seek, with every step,
to cancel out the dark.

No doubt, it's faith that lights the way,
held high by wisdom's hand;
we're drawn toward a nearing gate
into uncharted land.

Behind the Smile!

Then, forward strive and not surmise
we've lived our lives in vain;
if faith we keep, rewards we'll reap,
with lasting peace our gain.

Tho, peace be rarest treasure, true ...
one wonders, yet, as-well,
"What was it the foretellers told,
and to whom did they tell?"

(Ballad)

Cowrite w/Charlyne Zurick

"FREEDOM"

~ now ~

The broadest road to
Freedom

is

The one that releases us

from

The fears ...
The tyrannies ...
So imposed upon us

as

Children
Before we
Are capable

of

Mature judgment!

(Free Verse)

*"As a child ~ I was once free as a wheel,
spinning fast, going nowhere!"*

...— = GOTTA TRY = —...
~ perseverance ~

...-=•=-...

Life is too slow for those who wait
Too hard for those that cry,
Life is too easy for them that laugh
And, too short for they who die.

..•..

But love_____
For those who really care,
Showing their depth through life
With another the same to share.

..•..

Are truly happy people
Together, seeking the best,
Knowing the nature in earth
Grasping her full-grown breast.

..•..

Love remains too deep for those who shrug
Too confusing for they whom don't care why,
Love is here to help us grow
With hearts that need too much ... not to try!

...-=•=-...

(Unmetered Quatrains)

"The only absolutely, necessary factor for success?
Never give-up!"

Thinking

===GREATER~SELF===

~ to realization ~

~=+=~

You say you do not know me
That I am too difficult and hard to understand

But I say that I am within you

You have but to seek me in the correct way
Within the proper place

and

You shall find me there waiting for you....

~ within your own ~

===GREATER~SELF===

(Free Verse)

*"....all too often ~ we cannot know others, because we
are so self-absorbed
it is impossible to see ourselves in them...."*

I wonder, "Why?"

As morning wakes, I stir to sounds of life.
It's not the normal kind of life I hear,
but of an ilk that stirs the heart and soul;
a loveliness that cannot be denied.
How is it that I fall in-love with sound,
when songs of birds' sing melodies to me,
as crickets saw their hymnal mating rites,
and laughing children fill me full of joy?
Oft, times I've sat and questioned how I fit,
of what my purpose here on Earth may be;
and, then I look around and wonder why,
with all the beauty, why I even ask?

(Blank Verse)

— If This Makes Any Sense —

It's a happy song, come sing along ...
    to wherever we may go.
We'll dance and smile, and stay awhile;
    then, set the night aglow!

The big moon's high, romance is nigh,
    all 'round bright fireflies flit;
so, tip your glass, let sorrows pass,
    sweet vows of love commit.

Frogs are singing, vines a'swinging
    to a most happy tune.
Of poems sad, and those so glad,
    a hymn of each let's croon;

for, both it takes — for both their sakes;
    or, neither could exist.
How would we know of fast and slow ...
    if they did not persist?

Thus, if you're sad — you're also glad,
    in equal increments;
so, make that frown turn upside down,
    if this makes any sense.

(Eights 'n Sixes)

~ In Life's Review ~

Ah, my fate, how you so break me down...
from that imagined man I'd thought of me;
for, when you've returned to me a frown,
I see in me a man – I'd hoped, to never be.

~⎯⎯⎯⎯⎯~

When yon four winds have called my name
and all my stars no longer shine,
I'll know there's no one else to blame;
for, the blame to take ... is solely mine.

~⎯⎯⎯⎯⎯~

(Unmetered Quatrains)

In names unknown...

'Tis
cruel your man's feeling so bereft,
'cause him you've up and left
alone.

Now,
aching days that stretch too long unwind;
"You've treated me unkind!"
I groan.

Please,
unto me return with your sweet fire;
I'll lay 'pon your hot pyre
and moan.

For,
better burnt by your dark searing flames,
than search for you ... in names
unknown.

(Child Four)

INTERRUPTING!

Starting out, something, no doubt,
was on my mind to say;
but, every line I spoke of it ...
your voice got in the way.

I'm trying to move on by you,
but your mouth won't desist.
You've gone boring, I'm ignoring,
but guess you can't resist.

It drives me nuts, there are no buts
of how I really feel.
When I'm speaking, you start wreaking
your havoc on my zeal.

I even try to figure why
you persist disrupting.
Listening close, you gush verbose,
and keep interrupting.

If you agree with this, my plea;
please, never interrupt;
and, if you do this tact ensue,
watch then my ire erupt!

I'll close for now, making a vow,
to never try and share
another thing that's happening,
expecting you to care.

Never so rude, the interlude,
where one can't wait their turn;
and, bless'ed are...who hear by far,
they will, by list'ning – learn.

(Eights 'n Sixes)

~I~S~L~A~N~D~S~
~ loneliness ~

~
~~~
~~~~~~~
~~~~~~~~~~

We are all
# ISLANDS
shouting desperately

to one another

across vast

seas

of

mis

under

standing

~~~~~~~~~~
~~~~~~~
~~~
~

.

*"When unable to touch another's heart,
one can become very lonely; it is akin to being marooned
at sea with no fresh water, telling oneself it's okay
to sip the brine!"*

(Concrete)

JOY & HAPPINESS

~ what else? ~

Joy & Happiness....
it lives within us
those who have it, that is

Not one of us....
can seek and find

What....
is not already there inside

To....
be discovered and brought forth

This....
is true of everything that composes

LIFE

Because...
nothing can be derived from nowhere

... with no source ...

(Free Verse)

*"In the search for joy and happiness, seek no further,
for it dwells within us ~ where it's always been!"*

~ Karmic Relief ~

The strain of life depletes me more each day;
it seems there is no path that leads to ease.
With yearning hope, I pray to find a way ...
allowing true relief that will appease.

I've heard it told how karma leads to fate,
how each and every deed is recompensed;
yet, still, and furthermore, why does this weight,
thus borne, feel so unevenly immense.

While looking back on all of my foul deeds,
such truth begins to clearly come in view ...
with vivid colors every scene proceeds
into the next, 'til suddenly I knew;

I'd failed to heed and listen at each stage ...
until I do, life's pain will not assuage.

(English Sonnet)

•LIFE'S BRIGHT STREAM•

~ L'Chaim - To Life ~

—=•†•=—

Upon traversing the swirling tides of life
Much passes by unseen,
And if by chance we could live it all
It would surpass the most glorious dream.

—=•†•=—

There's the worldly life we carry within
Where daily thoughts and schemes unfold,
While only skimming the surface
Of realms that deeper longings hold.

—=•†•=—

One cannot know the essence of another's soul
Nor walk life's path upon another's feet,
One can only hope to venture forth and find
That which makes their own dreams complete.

—=•†•=—

Not one dream, but yet many
Shall seek their own fulfillment thine,
It is within each life experienced & found
Trying, trudging, toil the soul's bounty shall unwind.

—=•†•=—

Behind the Smile!

Times tempted toward self-righteous blight
Where we're left living life's driest scheme,
Yet, before we've grasped just why or how
We're swept back into "Life's Bright Stream"

What other choice life leaves for us
But through its nearest alluring gate,
Rightly knowing we must enter and learn
Or complacently must we sit and wait.

Birds & flowers & clouds that flow
Who's to teach when or what to love and feel,
What rules have the pen-in-hand yet written
That might change life's magnetic turning wheel.

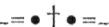

There are none, there are truly none
And, alas, I am most compelled to display,
These immersing ripples from "Life's Bright Stream"
As they warmly embrace us and swirl us away.

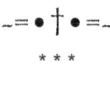

(Unmetered Quatrains)

"We seek, we question ~ slowly we unfold as flowers to the sun, gracing the world, each in our own way, in our own time."

Life's Slaves

A vassal, thrall, or bondsman, true we are;
some say, "A servant, lackey, minion, drudge,
adherent, devotee, to some slave tsar!"
All serving something, throughout life we trudge.
It may be work or to some art we're tied;
so many are addicted to a drug ...
then, far too often ruled by some set guide,
we follow blindly like a mindless slug.
Too many, slaves of cold brutality
that marriage to the wrong one locks away;
seems no escape from such despondency
when dragged while shackled, to their sad dismay.
Chained tight to something, whether man's or God's,
we're slaves, because we're all bound to life's odds.

(English Sonnet)

Behind the Smile!

Listen well, you who soar...!

Shhh, let's listen together closely!
Do you hear these silent voices that I do?
Heard in moments softly bright
they're rare and come to just a few.

I wish that all could hear them,
'cause they've beautiful things to say
about the world in which we live,
through our each and every day.

We're supposed to learn what it is (it seems)
makes the world go 'round;
to've been taught by the glorious wonder,
living in each sound.
I've listened, looked, perceived...
and, from it all, here is what I've found:

Far too many of us there are,
learned to live a life askew,
except those fortunate enough,
who know how to laugh and play,
soar to heights on wings of gold; yet,
keep both feet... firm on the ground.

(Cinq Trois Decca La)

...~.~* LISTEN *~.~...

· to my spirit speak ·

● · · · · · · · · · · · ●

● · · closer · ●

● · · · · · · · ●

can't you hear the ether call?
it beckons to you and me
come dwell within its
boundless shores
like drops we
merge into a
greater sea

● · · ● · · ●

can't you feel the ether here?
touch with all embracing
inner-glow

● · · · ●

Shhhh!

● · · ●

.~.~* LISTEN *~·~.

● · ●

*

·

(Free Style)
.~·~ In quietest moments, sometimes my spirit flies ~
my soul soars to nether places, otherwise unknown to me ~·~.

MORTALITY

Dance gaily ~ leaves upon life's wind.
Flow swiftly ~ rivers to sea blend.
Love softly ~ in life's every turn.
Eternity ~ I shall befriend.

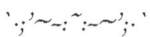

Enrichment ~ harvest joy's sweet song.
Endowment ~ honor makes us strong.
Acquiring ~ from wisdom we learn.
Tranquility ~ rest with no wrong.

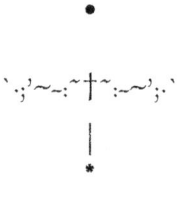

(Ruba'i)

On Life and Death

~ stepping into eternity ~

"From the unknown we come to the unknown we return,
brilliant flashes in the infinitely-ethereal!"

... the SUN ...
setting at one point ~ rises at another
Every moment in its motion
is an eternal, uninterrupted rising and setting.

For, as the sun
rises in its setting and sets in its rising,
... so is Life and Death ...

We die when we are born
and are born when we die

Death*Sunrise
Birth*Sunset

... all THESE ...
are but the thoughts, dreams, fears
of the
Blind and Sleeping;

for, all Life
is a death beginning,
and all Death,
a life continuing,

Neither, separate from the other.

(Free Verse)

In contemplation to the "impossibility"
of coming from nowhere and going to nowhere
~ with no source and no destination ~
this realization can bring great comfort from the loss
of those who have left us ...
that...
there has to be a somewhere else for Them ~ for Us.

-=ON-→MOTION=-
~ by way of words ~

"Imagine a single grain of sand for the moment"

~> . <~

~ One Grain In A World of Endless Multitudes ~

Imagine you're holding that grain between your fingers,
feeling its minuteness.

Now, in your mind's eye....
Picture the vast expanses of all the beaches
and deserts ever known.
The fact that this grain exists is diminished
not one iota in the presence of
even the overwhelming immensity of
the universes of grains of sand.

..•..

Should you drop this tiny grain of sand
into the surface of the ocean,
you can rest assured that the ocean
will amply expand to receive it,
and that "that" expansion has produced
some infinitely connected change
upon the entire universe.

.●*●.

In the presence of such a unique realization
and conscious dawning....

You can begin to grasp the effects and perpetuity
of the sources and reactions

of the magnitude of motions/energies that begin
infinitely smaller than your grain of sand

and reverberate outwardly and back upon you from the entire
universe.

.●*●.

All around and in you is motion....

Some within reach of your sight and touch,

and some are smaller or larger than you can perceive.

..°..

There is nothing...

..°..

Even in your entire composition,

that is not motion.

.●° | °●.

Even the energy of your emotion....

Is, in some abstract manner,

chained to this phenomenal action-reaction.

.●° | °●.

If not....

No energy for thought would exist as a result
of what you are reading.

However....

What "material-proof" can be offered to
substantiate this astonishing fact
meant only for your mind to grasp?

..•..

Yet....

..•..

By some unknown/un-provable process,
we are capable of grasping this concept of higher conscious
dawning.

What logical or scientific proof....

Can exist for what you are meant to know intuitively?

~=÷=~

The awareness....

Of love, hurt, hate, or any feeling you
experience is all motion

that has influenced you from some outside stimulus.

~=÷=~~=÷=~

-=Everything Is Motion=-

~=÷=~~=÷=~~=÷=~

This is the world that....

Although, invisible,

exists simultaneously with the one that's known
to your five-senses.

•

To know this world...

we must see it with our sixth-sense.

Our intuitive understanding of motion and energy
that is only visible to the mind's eye.
<•>
Where does....
the energy of intuitive-understanding of
thought by motion take you?
*
This has been but an exercise....
in realization of what an awakened mind sees,
and the quality of its active interest as compared with the, quote:
"... Normal world you would usually be involved in ..."
.
This has been....
-=The Invisible Motion of Conscious Thought=-

<====• made visible by way of words •====>
...•• * ••...
:

•

.

(Prose Poetry)

An Exercise in Conscious Thinking
"If you sit quietly ~ still all thought ~ shut-out all sound around
you, if it is free of effort, "the feel ~ the energy" of motion in you
and in all around you will be present to experience its wonder."

On • TRUTH
~ conclusion ~

_===§===_

From the unknown we emerge,
Through worlds beyond touch and view,
To now in this, the moment of conscious dawning
Where truth can only strive to shine through.

_==§==_

Some infinite vastness of nondescript energy
All stretching infinitely away,
This madness that comprehends nothing
Except, "On • TRUTH" we can only play!

_=§=_

_=_

*

.

(Unmetered Quatrains)

It is within the acceptance of this awakening understanding that I have found the greatest peace and cure for unknowable answers ~ and I suspect those upon the firmest ground have derived the same, or similar, conclusion that ...

"_=there is truth, Truth; and TRUTH=_"

Paradoxical Infatuation

To grasp all words e'er to exist,
would be to make an empty list.

Wanting to joyously skip in glee,
yet, there's no want inside of me.

Drink then thy wettest emotions,
tho' driest of deepest oceans.

Faster sliding down steepest hills,
near the top's no farther my thrills.

Whene'er within the throes of love,
all's there is hateful push and shove.

So, now you decided truth complies,
though, every line of this poem lies.

That's the rare rub in this conundrum,
paradoxical parallelismus memborum.

(Parallelismus Membrorum)

PATH OF CHOICES

These are troubled times my friend
In my mind I feel it's true,
With no means for an end
Nothing old, nothing new.

•

It's an uncertain time....Learning

No escape from a world of dreams
Of billowed clouds on high,
Passengers on Albatross wings
Wave their last good-bye.

•

It's a sad time....Leaving

Falling up is harder than falling down
The latter just hurts the most,
Work your sweat into the ground
Beat your head against that post.

•

It's a harder time....Doing

Sample this – taste the grit
The aftermath of grinding teeth,
Trip into a deep dark pit
Look up the scope to the sky's blue wreath.

•

It's a long way....Reaching

It's only you I'm looking for
Don't hide from me too long,
If you see a star that cannot shine
It's only me, for I've done wrong.

•

It's the shortest way....Loving!
... and ...
Caring enough to let go
when it's time.

(Unmetered Quatrains w/Refrains)

*The path to a better life and relationship
is often a trying and confusing one to navigate!*

"SELF-MADE MAN"
~ self-revealing moment ~

The sun never shines
On my shoulders these days,
As I stand I squint
In this solitude haze.

So I run like the wind
With the sun bearing down,
Like the speed of a fox
At the bay of a hound.

But I've chosen how fast
To run in this race,
Made my own stand
In this wet boggy place.

Yes, there'll never be a place for a sail in my life
For, I'd have to depend on the wind,
'Long this journey of self-made strife,
None's left but myself, who still calls me friend.

(Unmetered Quatrains)

"Before I knew how to love ... to give, and to share!"

"SOME KIND OF ADVICE"

...just talking...

If you have a good thing,
Share it with others
Who knows –
Someone might even need or appreciate it
If you don't have a good thing,
Then don't try to share it with others
No one will want it for long
Or You!
There is so much to be learned in this world
If learning is your bag
If it isn't?
Don't be too concerned
You can get by with just the basics
But only until you meet the world outside of your own
Then what will you do
When you meet a new experience?
I hope you aren't extremely naïve
It's so hard a task to teach
Where there's no knowledge at all
Almost like helping a child with its first step

(Prose Poetry)

= SUM = OF = INDUSTRY =

To take bread

from the mouths of free men

and endeavor to

regulate their pursuits,

is not a worthwhile, wise,

or

frugal labor.

(Prose)

~=+TAKE A GOOD LOOK+=~

~ measure-up ~

~= += + =~

There comes a time when each of us
must step back and take that good look,
Not fidget-around with himself
but tear the cover right off of that book.

= = =

Turn over each leaf carefully true
peel back those pages one by one,
Examine every line with scrutiny
no letter, syllable, or line left undone.

= = =

Every page numbered and accounted
in the sequence which it belongs,
One erroneous part that is discovered
must be added direct to the wrongs.

= = =

An accounting must be diligently
thoroughly and passionately made,
Table of content must be precise
glossary and index to make the grade.

= = =

Thinking

_= = =_

Words not allowed un-liked or abhorred
will not be approved and highly suspected,
Sentiments too passionate, too loving to bear
cause this entire book to be rudely rejected.

_~= ~=~ =~_

•
.

(Unmetered Quatrains)

There may come a time when you lose sight of just who you are ~
who you may have become ~
when a stepping-back must be done.. be accountable..
own what you find!

TEMPLE KNOWS
~ for thinkers - everywhere ~

Temple, the young man
grew strong and wise like the oak;
people gathered from miles around
to listen quietly while he spoke.

It was not so much his words
as what his message wrought;
he says, "We could gather in comfort only
if peace in our souls is what we brought,"

and that, "green pastures
are the brothers to us and trees ...
that people should breathe life's clean air
than this vile, inconceivable disease.

That, that which grows is life-itself,
and life, as love, can die too new;
what is warm in the protective night
can be gone, like morn's cold crystal dew!"

Then, they began to know why it's so lonely
when there's no love to warm inside ...
how life can be more wisely spent
in search of an inner peace borne guide.

"But, such is life for the defiant," he refrained,
"that have yet to know the barren wiles
of those whom we've heard speak tomes
for living the materially-accepted styles,

creating a lust for that so easily ignored ...
those wrongly-justified imbalances we see,
turning our backs on others' shackles
'We, The People' might have helped set free;

and, if we share part of what we know
to help uplift the weakened and guiled
to embrace those who know no love,
or furnish a ray of sunshine for a child.

If in just one purely-driven instance
we might realize this mere unselfish goal,
there would be one less heavy burden
weighing on our own life's sagging soul;

and, if there were more of us to give,
creating less greedy, reaching to receive,
we might refrain with more enduring love
o'er that goodness we profess to believe!"

_ _ _ _ _ _ _ _ _ _ _ _ † _ _ _ _ _ _ _ _ _ _ _ _

Temple fell silent then, lowered his head to sleep,
as darkness returned its oldness ...
the last drawn breath of evening's sun,
glittering leaves through moon-lit night ...
and they were strangely one;
perhaps, now only new, standing silently together
— until, one-by-one ...
each went their separate way............ ❖

_ _ _ _ _ _ _ _ _ _ _ _ † _ _ _ _ _ _ _ _ _ _ _ _

(Unmetered Quatrains w/Envoi)

~†~ THE ~ OTHER ~ WAY ~†~
~ seeking religious truth ~

~†~

Before these trails of vaporous longings
I walk this tired, tired road,
Through suns of newfound dawnings
Each adding profoundness to this, my weary load.

†

Through crystal eyes appears the world
Once void of these bright colors meant for me,
Until, then, within the midst of life I swirled
To seek in wonder where my soul might be.

†

"The Devil has it!" came one reply
Another said, "That's not true, at all!
Upon the light of faith you must fly
In answer to your soul's low mournful call!"

†

"There's a quiet place within you; true,
Where there's no confusion!" smiled the Devil,
"But, it's up the gold-paved road toward the blue!"
Replied the angel from its lofty-level.

†

‡

Scattered rays of blinding light
Began to fill and sear my inner-being,
"Kneel down! Kneel down, before My might!
For, it's God, Himself, that you are seeing!"

‡

"No! No!" replied a nondescript vile thing
"It's me before you, and Lucifer's the name!
Isn't the fire of the sun the vibrant heat I bring,
And isn't it from that heat all life's to blame?"

‡

In answer to these manifest spirits' debate
I clenched my teeth in agony and doubt,
Setting my delicately balanced soul ablaze
And screamed in fury, "You both, get out!"

‡

"You have taunted my being into long, hard flight!
Can't you see my feet are bound and sore,
That the sounds you make, so old and trite...
Inspire longing for peace I've not known before?"

‡

‡

"Fire is not for me, and neither is blind faith;
For, if there is only life to live, nay death to fear,
And no hell or gold paved streets to know!
Where I now dwell, there exists but now and here!"

‡

"There is no straighter path for me!" said I
"It exists only that I may come to see,
To grasp in all its glory this one answer:
That only Truth shall set my own soul free!"

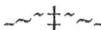

(Unmetered Quatrains)

....following years of study to determine Truth about religions, there being literally hundreds, each one professing to be THE answer, if one can only accept FAITH (those things fervently hoped for and believed-in, without the need for proof). I have concluded that, for me, there is no higher religion than TRUTH, whatever it may prove to be, wherever, whenever, however it is found....

The Secret of Love and Wisdom

To love is life renewed,

while life is eternally reborn ...

each love a countless treasure

of growing wisdom.

Hope for constant love.

(Prose)

Us ~

We know of life, we know of love,
the stars and universe above;

yet, what we know is minuscule,
who knows it all is a sad fool,

but what I see, I'll tell you true;
dwells all there is inside of you.

The galaxies, bright stars above,
lives in each mind, shines in our love.

If not for us, there would not be,
one planet far or galaxy.

Inscrutably, this thought's surreal,
through us life turns like a great wheel.

Colossally, from us comes all ...
to infinitesimally small.

Life's patterned from woman and man ...
life's scheme is Us ~ we are God's plan.

(Rhyming Couplets)

"CLOSING COMMENTS"

To You, my wonderful reader:

Thank you so very warmly, gratefully, and appreciatively for buying and reading this first edition of my book.

It has been a great pleasure to write for you, sharing these few original poems, specially selected from my private collection.

I sincerely hope you've found much enjoyment herein to keep in your mind, heart, and soul.

Please, be sure to share your book with family and friends, and let them know where they can order a copy for their own library, that they may enjoy it whenever they wish.

If you would like to comment on anything about my writing or this book, please, send a message to me at: RJinHouston@sbcglobal.net

I'll be sure to respond accordingly.

Bless and keep you safe and well.

~ UNTIL WE MEET AGAIN ~

Warmest smiles to one and all,
Richard W. Jenkins :)

The 52 Poetic Forms Composing This Book

Ameri-Sonnet

A form created by Richard W. Jenkins, 14 Feb, 2008

Composition: Fourteen lines of seven syllables each. [three quatrains and an ending couplet] Align left or centered, author's choice. Rhyme Scheme: abab/cdcd/efef/gg

Ballad

Centuries-old in practice, the composition of ballads began in the European folk tradition, in many cases accompanied by musical instruments. Ballads were not originally transcribed, but rather preserved orally for generations, passed along through recitation. Their subject matter dealt with religious themes, love, tragedy, domestic crimes, and sometimes even political propaganda.

Ballads began to make their way into print in fifteenth-century England. During the Renaissance, making and selling ballad broadsides became a popular practice.

Typically composed in Quatrains: 4-verses minimum, with no limit.

Meter: Iambic Syllable Counts: 8/6/8/6 Rhyme Scheme: abab, cdcd, etc; (or) abcb, defe, etc.

Blank Verse

Lines must not rhyme. There is no limit to number of lines. Each line is composed in iambic pentameter.* (*10-syllables in natural soft/HARD syllable cadence or flow)

Brady's Touch

Original form by Pamela (Gungalo) Jackson ©2011

Two 10-line verses minimum. Syllable counts of: 9 9 8 8 2 9 9 8 8 2 Rhyme scheme: a b x d e a b x d e

Chant Royal

One of the rarer French forms, the chant royal got its name because it was supposed to be sung before kings and its composition was considered worthy of royal honors. Actually a larger form of the ballade, it consists of five stanzas of eleven lines and an envoy of seven. Its purpose as well as its purport is serious, even solemn. The rhyme scheme for each verse is as follows:

ababccddedE The rhyme scheme for the envoy is: ccddedE

Chardelle

A form created by Charlyne "Char" Zurick, Oct 2009

6-lines per verse...two verse minimum. Syllable count...5 5 9 5 5 9. Rhyme scheme...aabccb, ddeffe, etc.

Char's 3+1

A form created by Charlyne "Char" Zurick, June 2012

This form requires 3 minimum 8-line verses with the following rules,

beginning with Verse 1, Line (1). Rhymes, Number of Syllables:
(1) a-a, 4-4
(2) b, 8
(3) c-c, 4-4
(4) d, 6
(5) e-e, 4-4
(6) f, 8
(7) g-g, 4-4
(8) h, 6
Etc...

Child Four

Created 06/23/2010, by Ethel (last name unknown)
Two verse minimum with no limit. Four lines per verse. Syllable count: 1, 9, 6, 2
Rhyme Scheme:: abbc, deec, fggc, hiic, etc; about anything.

Choka

Most intricate and versatile form of all Japanese poetry is the Choka (chock-uh), or Long Poem.
Two verse minimum, no limitation in numbers of verses; many have exceeded 100-lines.
Title, capitalization, and punctuation is allowed, though not required.
The Choka is unrhymed and structured 5-7-7-5-7-7, etc.
This form can be about anything.

Cinq Trois Decca La

At least one 10-line stanza. 15-syllables per line. Rhyme scheme: aa bb ccc abc

Concrete, Pattern, Form, Visual, or Shape Poetry

This style of poetry is an arrangement of linguistic elements in which the typographical effect is more important in conveying meaning than verbal significance. It is sometimes referred to as visual poetry, a term that has now developed a distinct meaning of its own. As such, concrete poetry relates more to the visual than to the verbal arts and there is a considerable overlap in the kind of product to which it refers. Historically, however, concrete poetry has developed from a long tradition of shaped poems in which the words are arranged in such a way as to depict their subject.

Crown of Sonnets

A Crown of Sonnets is a seven English Sonnet sequence with a single theme. Each Sonnet is written in iambic pentameter,, with the link to the preceding AND succeeding Sonnets AND the last line of each Sonnet becomes the first line of the next. To tie them all up in a bow, the first line of the first Sonnet is repeated once again – as the final line of the last Sonnet.

The 52 poetic forms composing this book

Cywydd Devair Fyrion
Another of the Welsh forms. This one has only four syllables per line.
Rhyming couplets. aa bb cc dd etc; no less than 10 stanzas,
but no limit to how many.

Diminished Hexaverse, Tetraverse, Pentaverse, Etc.
Diminished poetry begins with a verse containing however many lines the author chooses to begin.

For example: 10 = a beginning verse of ten 10-syllable lines, with every following verse one line and 1-syllable less per line, etc; until the final verse is "diminished" down to one 1-word line and verse.

End-line rhyming and rhyme scheme are the author's choice, but rhyming is not required.

Eights 'n Sixes
A form created by Richard W. Jenkins, © 1 Apr 1987.
Any number of 4-line verses about anything, 2 verse minimum.
Syllable count per verse: 4-4/6/4-4/6 Rhyme scheme: a-a b c-c b, d-d e f-f e, Etc...

Fives 'n Eights
A form created by Richard W. Jenkins, © 4 May 1987.
6 line verses, 2-verse minimum. Syllable counts: 5/5/8/5/5/8 5/5/8/5/5/8
Rhyme scheme: a/a/b/c/c/b d/d/e/f/f/e, Etc...

Fives 'n Tens
A form created by Richard W. Jenkins, © 8 July 1987.
6 line verses, 2-verse minimum, aligned left or centered.
Syllable counts: 5/5/10/5/5/810 5/5/10/5/5/10
Rhyme scheme: a/a/b/a/a/b c/c/d/c/c/d, Etc...

Fours 'n Eights
an original form by: Richard W. Jenkins Created: 16 Oct 1998
Rules: Unlimited quatrain verses with the following Counts: 4-4 8 4-4 8
With the following Rhyme Scheme:
a-a b a-a b, c-c d c-c d, Etc...

Free Style
Intermittent rhyming poetry without a set meter or count.
This is NOT a narrative or prose form ... must have a poetic voice.
Rhythm and word-flow decide where to place the rhymes.
Technically, this form is free verse with intermittent rhymes.

Behind the Smile!

Free Verse

Unrhymed poetry without a set meter or count, but must flow.

This is NOT a narrative or prose form ... must have a poetic voice, spoken with rhythm and word-flow, and thoughts grouped, with appropriate line-breaks and enjambments.

Freud Style

An eight verse minimum poem, composed of unrhymed, three-syllable, three line verses ... no minimum to numbers of verses, but must be about deep thought, romance, emotion, or, with a philosophical bent, and may be sensual, sexual. or erotic, but is not required to be

Haiku

An unrhymed Japanese poem recording the essence of a moment. Has a Nature Theme. It usually consists of three lines of 5/7/5 syllables, without punctuation or capitalization, and no formal title ... though, a one, two, or three word mention of it's essence is tolerable. Each line of the Haiku must stand alone as its own statement without enjambment. Line 1 sets the scene or the mood, Line 2 describes the scene, and Line 3 concludes with a powerful solution, or message.

scene/mood (5-syllables)

meaning/description (7-syllables)

solution/message (5-syllables)

Kyrielle

The Kyrielle is a French form written in quatrains. Each quatrain contains a repeated line or phrase as a refrain. It has a meter usually composed of eight syllables per line but it can be varied. There is no limit to the number of stanzas, but three is generally the minimum.

The normal structure is a/a/b/B, c/c/b/B, d/d/b/B. with B being the repeated line. A varied structure could be a/b/a/B, c/b/c/B, d/b/d/B. etc. or even a second line that did not rhyme at all. a/e/a/Z etc.

Limerick (in general)

A limerick is a humorous poem consisting of five lines.

The first, second, and fifth lines must have seven to ten syllables, while rhyming and having the same verbal rhythm. The third and fourth lines only have to have five to seven syllables, and have to rhyme with each other and have the same rhythm.

Limerick (English)

A humorous poem of five lines with a rhyme scheme of a-a-b-b-a

Lines 1, 2, and 5 have a syllable-count of nine, while lines 3 and 4 have six-syllables each.

Mollietta

An original form created by: Mollie Reckitt ©2006

Rules: Of a Nature theme.

Each verse has ten syllables in three lines. Rhyming is author's choice.

Mono-Rhyme

is a rhyme scheme in which each line, or a series of three lines or more, has an identical rhyme.

The term "Mono-rhyme" describes the use of one (mono) type of repetitious sound (rhyme), usually at the end of each line, but sometimes spread throughout the poem.

Ottava Rima

Format:

Ten syllables per line.

Line 1 - rhyme a
Line 2 - rhyme b
Line 3 - rhyme a
Line 4 - rhyme b
Line 5 - rhyme a
Line 6 - rhyme b
Line 7 - rhyme c
Line 8 - rhyme c

Pantoum

The Pantoum is a poetic form derived from the pantum, a Malay verse form. Specifically from the pantum berkait, a series of interwoven quatrains from the 15th century, a short folk poem.

The Pantoum is similar to the Villanelle, in that there are repeating lines throughout the poem. It is composed of a series of 5 quatrains in lines of 8-syllables each; the 2nd and 4th lines of each stanza are repeated, as the 1st and 3rd lines of the next stanza, as follows:

Line 1 - Rhyme A
Line 2 - Rhyme B
Line 3 - Rhyme A
Line 4 - Rhyme B
Line 5 - Line 2 previous verse B
Line 6 - Rhyme C
Line 7 - Line 4 previous verse B
Line 8 - Rhyme C
Line 9 - Line 2 previous verse C
Line 10 - Rhyme D
Line 11 - Line 4 previous verse C
Line 12 - Rhyme D
Line 13 - Line 2 previous verse D
Line 14 - Rhyme E
Line 15 - Line 4 previous verse D
Line 16 - Rhyme E

Continue the cycle carrying the even lines to the odd of the next stanza for as many stanzas as you wish - though, with a minimum of four stanzas and a final Quatrain, as below:

EXCEPT FOR the last stanza which is built as follows:

Behind the Smile!

Line 2 of previous stanza E
Line 3 of FIRST stanza A
Line 4 of previous stanza E
Line 1 of FIRST stanza A

Parabolic Quatrains

a form created by Richard W. Jenkins © June 27, 2011

Five Quatrains in lines of 8-count each, with the beginning of each line indented right one click more below the title from line 1 through line ten, and one click left indent left from line twelve through line 20, lines ten and eleven of equal indent, creating a parabolic presentation.

Rhythm is in iambic tetrameter. Rhyme Scheme: abab, cdcd, efef, ghgh, ijij.

Parallelismus Membrorum

Parallelismus Membrorum is of traditional Hebrew origin.

It has at least two (or any number of) short lines of parallel construction that present a thesis and a complementary antithesis as extension. Parallelism means to give two or more parts of the sentences a similar form, so as to give the whole a definite pattern. For excellent examples of Parallelismus Membrorum, see the Biblical book of "Proverbs."

Primetime

An original form: Created by Charlyne "Char" Zurick

© 06/24/2010 Minimum of 4 verses. Three lines per verse. Syllable count 7/7/10. Rhyme Scheme a a b c c b   d d b   e e b Please, note the rhyme for each of the third lines is the same. Any theme or length. Center-aligned.

Prose

Ordinary language people use in speaking or writing, as distinguished from the heightened language of poetry. In prose, the line is not treated as a formal unit and has no line breaks or enjambment, nor does it employ the repetitive patterns of rhythm or meter associated with many forms of poetic expression. Sidelight: The cadence of artistic or rhythmical prose is not pre-established, but emerges from the rhythm of thought and it's free expression.

Prose Poem

A genre in the poetic spectrum between free verse and prose. It is distinguished by the poetic characteristics of rhythmic, aural, and syntactic repetition, compression of thought, sustained intensity, and patterned structure, but is set on the page in a continuous sequence of sentences as in prose, without line breaks.

Quatern

A Quatern is a sixteen line French form, composed of four Quatrains. It is similar to the Kyrielle and the Retourne. It has a refrain that is in a different place in each quatrain. The first line of stanza one is the second line of stanza two, third line of stanza three, and fourth line of stanza four. A Quatern has eight syllables per line. It does not have to be iambic or follow a set rhyme scheme.

line 1

line 2

line 3
line 4

line 5
line 6 (line 1)
line 7
line 8

line 9
line 10
line 11 (line 1)
line 12

line 13
line 14
line 15
line 16 (line 1)

Quatrain

Four line stanzas of any kind, rhymed, metered, or otherwise; there are many variations of the quatrain.

Quickie

A form created by Richard W. Jenkins, © 19 Apr 1987.
Any number of 6-line verses about anything: Align left or center.
Syllable count per verse: 4/4/6/4/4/6 Rhyme scheme: aabccb, ddeffe, etc…

Rhopalic Verse

Having each succeeding unit in a poetic structure longer than the preceding one.
Applied to a line, it means that each successive word is a syllable longer that its predecessor.
What form composed in, number of words in each line, meter, and rhyme is each the writer's choice.

Rhyme Royal

Rhyme royal (or Rime Royal) is a rhyming stanza form that was introduced into English poetry by Geoffrey Chaucer. The rhyme royal stanza consists of seven lines in iambic pentameter. The rhyme scheme is a-b-a-b-b-c-c. In practice, the stanza can be constructed either as a Tercet and two couplets (a-b-a, b-b, c-c) or a quatrain and a Tercet (a-b-a-b, b-c-c). This allows for variety, especially when the form is used for longer narrative poems, such as the Canterbury Tales. Along with the couplet, it was the standard narrative metre in the late Middle Ages.

Behind the Smile!

Rhyming Couplets

A pair of lines that have the same meter (syllable-counts), which share the same end rhyme, allowing them to flow comfortably, appealingly, and harmoniously.

Rubiyat or Ruba'i

This Arabic format has a quatrain wherein the first, second, and fourth lines rhyme. The rhyme scheme is thus; a-a-b-a. A single stanza can be a poem in itself or multiple stanzas may be joined to create a larger piece. Eight syllables per line.

Sedoka

The Sedoka is an unrhymed poem made up of two three-line Katauta with the following syllable counts: 5/7/7, 5/7/7. Each Katauta addresses the same subject from opposite perspectives.

Senryu

An unrhymed Japanese poem recording the essence of a moment. Has a Human Theme, often humorous. It usually consists of three lines of 5/7/5 syllables, without punctuation or capitalization, and no formal title ... though, a one, two, or three word mention of it's essence is tolerable. Each line of the Haiku must stand alone as its own statement without enjambment. Line 1 sets the scene or the mood, Line 2 describes the scene, and Line 3 concludes with a powerful solution, or message.

scene/mood (5-syllables)

meaning/description (7-syllables)

solution/message (5-syllables)

Sonnet

(Little Song)

This is probably the most well known and recognized poetic format in the present day

Though, made famous by Shakespeare, this form is much older than his.

Sonnets are composed in fourteen lines. Note that the sonnet is traditionally written with no spaces between stanzas, but modern composers of sonnets often break their verses into three quatrains and a separated heroic couplet ending or separate only the heroic couplet.

Sonnet lines are composed in iambic pentameter: 10-syllables or 5 poetic feet, composed in iambic (soft/HARD) beat, tempo, rhythm, or meter.

Here is the rhyme scheme of the English (Shakespearean) Sonnet used in this book:

Verse 1: a-b-a-b Verse 2: c-d-c-d Verse 3: e-f-e-f Heroic Couplet: gg

Spilling Ink

Created by Jenny "Inkling" Buzzard ©2010

Spilling Ink takes a minimum of three stanzas, at eight lines per stanza,

with a syllable count of 8, 8, 8, 6, 8, 8, 8, 6.

Properly punctuated and centered, it takes the following rhyme scheme:

aaxbccxb, ddxeffxe, ggxhiixh

Swap Quatrain

Within the Swap Quatrain each stanza in the poem must be a quatrain (four lines) where the first line is reversed in the fourth line. In addition, line 2 must rhyme with line 1, and line 3 must rhyme with line 4 and so on, BUT not repeat the same rhyming pattern on subsequent stanzas. Eight syllables per line. Rhyming pattern: AABB, CCDD, and so on.

Tanka

The typical lyric poem of Japanese literature, composed of five unrhymed metrical units of 5,7,5,7,7 'sound symbols'; Tanka in English have generally been in five lines with a total of thirty-one syllables, often observing a short, long, short, long, long pattern. Tanka usually need no titles, though in Japanese a 'topic' (dai) is often indicated where a title would normally stand in Western poetry. In Japan, the Tanka is well over twelve hundred years old (haiku is about three hundred years old), and has gone through many periods of change in style and content. But it has always been a poem of feelings, often involving metaphor and other figurative language (not generally used in haiku). While Tanka praising nature have been written, and seem to resemble "long haiku," most Tanka deal with human relationships or the author's situation. The best Tanka harmonizes the writer's emotional life with the elements of the outer world used to portray it.

Tenz 'n Eightz

A new form created by Charlyne Zurick ©2013

Must be written in Iambic Pentameter Line syllable count: 10/8/8/10.

Rhyme Scheme: a/b/b/a, a/c/c/a, etc; (lines 1 and 4 must have the same rhyme in every verse).

Two verse – minimum.

Tenz on Twelve

An original form created by Charlyne Zurick ©2013

Four lines to a stanza, 2-stanza minimum. Syllable count: 10/10/10/12

Rhyme Scheme: a b c a / a b c a, etc. Tempo: iambic meter

Tripps O'er Quads

A true Mono-rhymed end-line form of three Quatrain verses minimum, where the first three lines of each verse are 6-syllables and the last line 4 & 4-syllables, with all end-lines and the 4&4 lines all the same rhyme sound as follows: a,a,a,a-a a,a,a,a-a a,a,a,a-a.

Two-Step

A smooth, quick tempo form of four verses minimum about anything.

Tempo: Iambic tetrameter Rhyme Scheme: xxaA etc; with the A line of each verse repeating

Villanelle

In a traditional Villanelle:

*The lines are grouped into five Tercets and a concluding quatrain. Thus a Villanelle has 19 lines.

*Lines may be of any length.

The Villanelle has two rhymes. The rhyme scheme is aba, with the same end-rhyme for every first and last line of each Tercet and the final two lines of the quatrain.

Two of the lines are repeated:

Behind the Smile!

1. The first line of the first stanza is repeated as the last line of the second and the fourth stanzas, and as the second-to-last line in the concluding quatrain.
2. The third line of the first stanza is repeated as the last line of the third and the fifth stanzas, and as the last line in the concluding quatrain.

Thus the pattern of line-repetition is as follows:

A1 b A2
a b A1
a b A2
a b A1
a b A2
a b A1 A2

In the above:

* The lines of the first Tercet are represented by "A1 b A2", because the first and third lines rhyme and will be repeated later in the poem.
* The first line of each subsequent stanzas is shown as "a" because it rhymes with those two lines.
* Meanwhile the second line ("b") is not repeated but the second line of each subsequent stanzas rhymes with that line.7

About the Poet

Richard W. Jenkins, celebrated poet laureate to a number of global poetry and writing sites, is a "poet's poet."

He began his love for poetry at the age of nine, when his aunt, an avid classical poet, gifted him his first taste of poetry by teaching him the English (Shakespearean) Sonnet.

Over the years, Richard has studied all aspects of poetry, becoming extensively educated and skilled in a wide variety of poetical styles and formats, passing along his knowledge and expertise to many. He has even created popular and widely used poetic forms of his own.

Richard has finally agreed to release a few of his thousands of treasured writings for publication.

Among his compositions, you will find much to relate to, to deeply enjoy and enthrall you. His poetry will surprise and take you on many amazing and enthralling journeys.

Fresh Ink Group

Publishing
Free Memberships
Share & Read Free Stories, Essays, Articles
Free-Story Newsletter
Writing Contests

⁂

Books
E-books
Amazon Bookstore

⁂

Authors
Editors
Artists
Professionals
Publishing Services
Publisher Resources

⁂

Members' Websites
Members' Blogs
Social Media

FreshInkGroup.com
Email: info@FreshInkGroup.com
Twitter: @FreshInkGroup
Google+: Fresh Ink Group
Facebook.com/FreshInkGroup
LinkedIn: Fresh Ink Group
About.me/FreshInkGroup

www.ingramcontent.com/pod-product-compliance
Lightning Source LLC
Chambersburg PA
CBHW070527090426
42735CB00013B/2883